a
Second
Chance
at
Heaven

a Second Chance *at* Heaven

MY SURPRISING JOURNEY THROUGH HELL, HEAVEN, AND BACK TO LIFE

TAMARA LAROUX

EMANATE
BOOKS

While the author openly shares her attempt at ending her life, she in no way condones suicide as an answer to life's problems. Rather, she shares her experience as a testimony to God's love and faithfulness even in the most difficult situations. If you are wrestling with anxiety, we recommend reaching out to a family member, close friend, pastor, or counselor for help. If you need further help, please call the National Suicide Prevention Lifeline: Call 1-800-273-8255.

Remember, you are loved with an everlasting love.

Contents

Publisher's Note

To share or not to share?

Sharing your story is never easy.

Sharing a story about seeing the afterlife is even harder. And that is precisely what Tamara Laroux has done in these pages. It took courage.

In *A Second Chance at Heaven* you will meet a normal girl on an abnormal day. She was no more special than you or me, but she had reached a desperate point in her life and felt she had nowhere to turn.

Tamara's experience at the crossroads of decision reminds me of one of the most famous lines ever uttered on the stage: "To be, or not to be: that is the question." Many English-speaking people on planet earth remember Hamlet's words from Shakespeare's play. Why? Because we identify with his dilemma.

The young Hamlet remains suspended in time between a world of pain and a world unknown. If he stays, he will have to confront his father's killer. If he goes, he will enter what he later calls an "undiscovered country," life on the other side of life. The stakes are high.

As we read on, Hamlet stays and fights through to the end. There are times in life we find ourselves at this same juncture, feeling the same way. *What should I do? Which way should I go?* For a young teenager named Tamara, that hour of decision and her response forever changed the way she sees life, death, and the love of God.

Today Tamara faces a different dilemma. To share or not to share?

It's hard to know what to do with experiences with the afterlife. If you are the type of person who needs the approval of others, you may shy away from sharing an extraordinary heavenly experience with anyone. If you have a daring personality, however, you run the risk of alienating most of your family and friends.

There is a Bible story that illustrates this same issue. In John 9, the author records the moment Jesus healed a man born blind. When the man received his sight, he naturally rejoiced. Nevertheless, when the Pharisees became aware of it, they immediately begin to cross-examine this newly healed man. They even dragged in his parents for questioning. Yet, the man could not help but rejoice and tell the truth about who healed him, impervious to his prosecutor's questions. This man knew no better than to celebrate the miracle that had just opened his eyes for the first time. He was forever changed. And he knew exactly who was responsible.

Yet his prosecutors worked hard to make him capitulate, deny, and even lie if necessary. He remained undeterred in the face of fear, intimidation, manipulation, and coercion.

Dare we share what Jesus has done for us? What are the consequences? What are the consequences if we do not? Like the man born blind, Tamara Laroux is one of many people who have encountered Jesus in a supernatural way, only to return to an inhospitable environment.

This is the dilemma Tamara—and many others—face today. If they share, they will face criticism. If they do not, they will be withholding valuable information. And that would be the ultimate irony, wouldn't it? Meeting the God of the universe and never telling anyone about him. Doesn't everyone have a right to know? Isn't it our job to tell others about him?

As her family and friends were challenged by her testimony, Tamara's testimony would run the same gauntlet as the man in John's gospel. In the end, however, Tamara's faith in the glorious goodness of our Creator compelled her to speak up and spread the good news, whatever might come. Tamara learned what it means to be brave and has become an inspiration to us all.

By no means is a dramatic experience with God a requirement of faith or believing. In fact, after his resurrection, Jesus said: "Thomas, because you have seen Me, you have believed. Blessed are those who have not seen and yet have believed" (John 20:29 NKJV).

Most of us will not see the afterlife before our life on

earth is done, and yet we can all know God's indescribable goodness through simple faith. Let Tamara's journey inspire you to believe that he is there and that he cares deeply for you.

To share or not to share? Like Hamlet, we will face difficult decisions. Like the man born blind, we have no other choice but to rejoice and share and offer others a similar opportunity to experience God's amazing love.

The stakes are too high.

Joel Kneedler
Publisher
Emanate Books

ONE

The Day I Died

The day I died began like any other West Texas morning in late September.

When I awoke, I had no idea I would later try to take my own life and experience an astounding supernatural journey. For the glory of God I'm compelled to tell that story to a society that often glamorizes and dramatizes suicide in TV and movies.

God can bring healing out of even the worst of days. In fact, what became the most extraordinary day of my life started like one of the most ordinary.

———

My alarm went off, and I immediately got up and raised the blinds. Outside the air-conditioned comfort of my

1

bedroom, it was already sultry, the rising sun simmering on the horizon like an egg sizzling in a skillet. I brushed my teeth and hopped into the shower. Hot and dry outside again. A quiz in algebra. Just another typical day.

I had just started my sophomore year at Permian High School in Odessa, Texas, home of the Panthers. If you recognize Permian from *Friday Night Lights*, the bestselling book later written about our championship football program that went on to inspire a movie and TV series, you immediately understand many aspects of my world at that time. My parents had met in Odessa and moved to El Paso after they married. Then my mom returned to Odessa after their divorce when I was about four. Even though West Texas was all I knew, I liked it there. Like many small communities, we prided ourselves on conservative values and liberal enthusiasm for local sports and homemade barbeque.

My life looked good—my life *was* good—for most of those fifteen years leading up to that fateful day. My family wasn't rich, but we were fairly well-off by small-town-Texas standards. My father worked as a top executive for a major clothing manufacturer, and many of our relatives enjoyed dividends from investments in oil and gas. My uncle owned a big ranch nearby and all of us cousins enjoyed riding horses, racing four-wheelers, and tanning by the pool there. We weren't the Ewings of *Dallas*, but I had definitely experienced moments of their lifestyle.

I had no logical reason to want to die that day.

———

Most people seemed to like me. Quiet and a little shy, I was considered a nice girl, well-mannered and from a good family. Many people told me I was pretty and complimented me on my honey-blonde hair and brown eyes. Based on remarks from some of the cruder boys at school, I knew my figure had matured with the curves of a woman, despite how much I still felt like a little girl. Even though I didn't feel pretty, like most teenage girls of the eighties, I spent way too much time curling my shoulder-length hair and applying my makeup like an artist with a blank canvas.

That day I wore my standard uniform, a pair of Levis and a T-shirt with "Go Panthers!" on it, along with my new pair of back-to-school Nikes. Giving my bouncy curls one last shake, I dabbed on a little more strawberry lip gloss and headed out of the room.

"Good morning, honey," Mom called as I entered the kitchen. "You want some eggs? Or I can make you a waffle if you—"

"Thanks, Momma," I said. "Not really hungry yet."

"Most important meal of the day." She turned on the TV in the living room and returned to the kitchen to pour herself a glass of coke. "You got to eat something, Tam."

Because she insisted, I nibbled a piece of toast with jam made with peaches from our giant tree in the backyard, the pride and joy of my green-thumbed mother. As I gathered my textbooks and homework into my backpack, the morning

3

news jumped from a sound bite of President Reagan talking about the AIDS crisis to an engineer commenting on the crash of a Delta jetliner near Dallas that summer.

"I want to hear this," Mom said and turned up the volume, eager to know if the cause had been determined for the tragedy claiming more than a hundred lives. Such news was personal for us. Her husband and my stepfather, Bill, was a pilot, and although he flew private jets chartered by wealthy oilmen, we still worried about his safety in the air.

As the news story ended, I asked, "When does Dad get back?" I had been calling Bill my dad from the time we moved back to Odessa after the divorce.

"Late tonight," Mom said. "Just a quick trip to Houston and back. Am I still picking you up after school or are you riding with Lori?"

As if on cue, my friend pulled into our driveway and tooted her horn. Lori was only a few months older than me, but she already had her license—and a mom willing to lease a candy-apple red Mustang for her only daughter. Lori and I had grown up together and now enjoyed the companionable sisterhood that teenage girls commit to with one another to avoid being the loner sitting on the bus or in the cafeteria by herself. We mostly talked about school or hot guys—my mom said Lori was "boy crazy"—or who sat with whom at the football game and what they wore.

Although I might have said Lori was my best friend at the time, the truth was I didn't have a best friend. I was too afraid of letting anyone see the real me. If my insecurities, imperfections, and self-doubts were more than I could handle, how could anyone else bear them? I was well-liked and got along well with most kids—jocks, stoners, nerds, band kids, even cheerleaders. So I hung out with a number of different friends and floated on the surface of life, never venturing beyond the shallow end of our emotional pool. We had a good time and shared lots of laughs, but that was it.

They had no idea about the weight of darkness crushing my heart.

"Gotta go," I called over my shoulder as I rushed out the door. "Bye, Mom!"

"Have a good day, honey," she said while unloading the dishwasher. "I'll see you at three."

———

Looking back now, I see the rest of that day blurring together in a collage of everyday moments made all the more poignant by my date with eternity. It was as if the surface version of my life—the life based on what I said and did, how I looked and where I spent my time—had collided with my interior world of pain, despair, and overwhelming hopelessness. My emotional avalanche had been building for some time, trying to pull me under, but I had always managed to dig my way out.

But no longer. That day, I was faced with all those feelings of isolation and loneliness, of not belonging or fitting in with any of the hundreds of kids walking the halls around me, of rejection and abandonment by people who said they loved me. It was too much. Like holding on to the chin-up bar in PE and feeling the muscles in my arms quiver before I had to let go, I could no longer bear the weight of my own pain.

If this sounds like the melodramatic angst of an overly sensitive teenage girl, please forgive me. But I'm not sure how else to describe that day to you. In many ways, it was just another day at school. Discussing *Hamlet* in Mrs. Collins's English class. Solving equations for unknown variables in algebra. Going to lunch off campus as a group of us piled into Lori's car and headed to Taco Bell. The only warning sign came while sitting in study hall during my free period.

In the school library that afternoon, it was as if a new awareness seeped into my consciousness. In the past I had always told myself that things would get better. That my life would change and someday I would be happy. I would leave Odessa and go to college, start an exciting career, meet someone special, and get married. He and I would travel to exotic places together, then start our family, and I would be fulfilled, secure in the knowledge that I was known and loved and free to love others without fear of being hurt.

But sitting at a table in study hall, I looked out the window and saw the truth.

My circumstances weren't the problem. I had a good life despite how depressed and alone I felt. My family loved me. My friends all liked me. My life, my family, school—none of them was the problem.

I was the problem.

And without thinking about it, I knew what I had to do. If I was the problem, I had no hope of ever escaping the unbearable weight shattering my soul. No matter where I went or what I did, I would never be able to outrun my own inadequacy. There was no hope. Nothing would ever change. The ache would only continue to wrack my heart. But I couldn't bear that thought because then there was no hope. No relief. No comfort. No happiness.

That was it.

I was done.

———

"How was your day, Tam?" Mom asked as I got in the car that afternoon.

"Okay—fine," I said, tossing my backpack behind me.

"You have much homework?"

I shook my head and gazed out the window as we pulled away from campus. The late-afternoon sky looked dreamy and autumn-blue, a hazy shade you only get in Texas in the fall. A few white clouds floated like tufts of cotton batted by the lingering jet stream of some long-gone plane.

I would miss it, the simple beauty of a lazy afternoon. But my decision had already been made. I had accepted it without any desire to reconsider. Just knowing my pain would be over soon already brought relief.

As we passed the football field, I saw the team practicing and envied the players' passion and determination for winning a game that seemed meaningless to me. And it wasn't just the players—the coaches and teachers, parents and neighbors, everyone cared so much about our football team and its record. The Panthers had won the state championship the year before, as well as several times before then, and although the season had barely started, the pressure to win was already enormous. As if any of it really mattered.

"You're awfully quiet today," Mom said. "Everything okay?"

I fought back tears as we pulled into our driveway. Our ranch-style house featured pale reddish-brown brick framed by shutters and trim painted a bright sun yellow. All I had to do was say I lived in the yellow house, and anybody in the area knew where it was. The weeping willow on the corner swayed in the breeze as if crying for me. And then I heard Foxy, our beloved Sheltie, barking from within the house, eager to see me and lick my face with her usual after-school greeting.

"Just tired, I guess."

Mom nodded and patted my knee. "I baked some banana bread today if you want a snack. I'm going to work in the yard for a little while if you need me. Have to cut back that honeysuckle before it jumps the fence."

"Thanks, Momma," I said, aware it would be the last time I'd see her or hear her lovely Texas drawl. "I . . . I love you." My voice began to tremble and I grabbed my backpack and hurried into the house. I didn't look back for fear she would ask more questions, but she was already headed toward her gardening shed.

Walking inside, I inhaled that unmistakable, familiar scent that I had come to take for granted. Fresh and citrusy from the lemon cleaner my mother used every day on our tiled entryway, mingled with clean laundry and a wisp of my mother's perfume, all wrapped in the divine smell of fresh-baked bread coming from the kitchen. I sighed, savoring that moment.

Eager for my attention, Foxy wagged her tail and ran around my feet until I petted her and let her lick my face. I hugged her close and then let her out the back door to chase squirrels in the backyard where Mom had just started trimming the vines laced around the old fence behind our peach tree. They both looked happy.

It was all more than I could bear.

———

I could no longer contain my awareness of what I was about to do. In my room with the door shut, I let the tears fall as I looked around at the clothes, books, CDs, and pictures, all the souvenirs of my life. A neatly folded stack of clean clothes Mom had placed on my dresser. The birthday card Dad had sent me that year. A bottle of drugstore perfume that matched the body wash in my shower. A ticket stub from the ballgame last Friday night. A small stuffed pink bear from last Valentine's day. A silly cartoon a friend had drawn for me the first day of school. Some loose change in a china teacup painted with roses.

"*You don't have to do this,*" a voice inside me said.

I ignored it, maintaining my resolve, and fumbled through the pages of an old notebook. I knew I wanted to write something to leave behind, but what could I possibly say to explain what I was about to do? More tears streamed down my cheeks. The last thing I wanted to do was hurt my family, but I couldn't go on. Mom would be so wrecked. But I knew her grief would fade over time.

Grabbing a pen, I sat on the floor by my bed and began to write in the neat curly script that any of my family and friends could identify as distinctly mine. "You have such pretty penmanship, Tamara," my elementary school teachers had always told me. Even though I now can't remember any of the words I committed to paper that day, I know without a doubt there was nothing pretty about them.

By the time I finished writing the second page, my hand was shaking. I didn't dare to reread it because I knew I would want to revise it. I wrote from my heart, and it would have to do. Where to leave it? On the kitchen table? On my dresser? Should I tear out the pages or leave them in the spiral-bound notebook? Closing the cover, I noticed some of the words had smeared from where my tears splattered the ink. I placed the notebook under my bed.

Just as I was about to leave my room, something caught my eye on the bedside table that made me cry even harder— the Bible my granny had given me. The thought of her softened my heart. While our family had gone to church on and off, I knew without a doubt there was a God because of my grandmother, my mom's mom. She was the best person I knew, always even-keeled and kindhearted, eager to ask me questions and listen beyond the short answers I usually gave her. Granny often told me about God's love and forgiveness, about his Son, Jesus, who left heaven to save us from our sins.

I had no doubt she believed every word she told me, and I envied the depth and intensity of her faith. But she might as well have been speaking a foreign language, because I didn't know what to do with what she said. I heard her, but I didn't understand her. I couldn't connect the dots between God's love and all the pain I felt inside, and all the suffering in the world. I had no doubt he existed, but I didn't know what difference that really made in my life.

But thinking of my granny made me cry harder. If I was about to find out what happens after you die, shouldn't I try to ask God for his forgiveness? After all, I knew taking my own life was wrong. But surely a God of love would show me mercy. I couldn't imagine him wanting any of his children to suffer with the unbearable weight I carried. Surely, he would forgive me, wouldn't he? I fell to my knees then, just like when I was a little girl saying prayers at bedtime.

"God, forgive me—please, *please* forgive me," I sobbed aloud.

When I got up, I heard Foxy barking and looked out my window. She was chasing her tail, and I couldn't help but smile. My mother was pulling weeds along the fence-row now. Shards of late afternoon sunlight cut through that still-perfect blue sky.

Leaving my room, I glanced back to make sure the notebook was still peeking out from beneath my bed. My tears hadn't stopped. I felt nothing at all. But suddenly: *What was that sound—did someone just come in the house?* Both my sister and brother were away. Mom was outside. Bill was at work. I froze in the hallway, grateful I was in my socks so I could move quietly, and listened. There it was again.

———

I stood there holding my breath. Nothing—just the house creaking. Foxy barking outside. Wind rustling through the evergreens at the other end of the yard.

Down the hall, I stood in the doorway to the master bedroom where Mom and Bill slept. Immaculate as always, the room looked like a page out of a magazine with a beautiful floral comforter and a half-dozen pillows on the king-size bed. I went to the right side of the bed, Mom's side, and opened the drawer of her nightstand.

Seeing the .38 revolver she always kept there—protection when Bill's job kept him away overnight—both startled and relieved me, like lifting a rock to find the snake you know is there. I was certain the .38 was loaded but checked to be sure. I wasn't about to play Russian roulette and chicken out because the gun's chamber was empty. This wasn't a half-hearted attempt or some cry for attention.

My mind was made up.

I went into the master bath and locked the door behind me. The heft of the gun in my hand felt cool and comfortable. I had already considered logistics and, ironically, knew I wanted to make this as easy as possible for Mom and Bill. I would be causing enough trouble and heartache without making a big mess on top of it. If I did it in the tiled shower stall, the cleanup would be much easier.

I stood in the shower and lifted the gun to my head.

"*Lower the gun to your heart,*" a voice inside said.

"No," I insisted. "I'm not taking any chances of living through this."

"*Spare your family as much as possible,*" the voice said. "*You don't want them to see you this way. If you want to make this easier on them, lower the gun to your heart.*"

I paused and envisioned the scene about to follow if I kept the barrel to my temple. A bullet through my head would make sure I got the job done, but it would also be a grisly sight for my loved ones. Blood and tissue would be splattered all over the tiles and half my face would be gone.

"Okay," I said and lowered my right arm, turning my hand in toward my left side. "I don't want them to suffer any more than they have to." The metal barrel felt like someone's finger poking me in the chest. My heart fluttered and throbbed like a bird escaping her cage. I was about to be free.

"God, forgive me," I whispered. "Please forgive me, Lord!"

I gently placed my finger on the trigger and thought about pulling it. But I didn't have to. Immediately the gun fired into my chest.

TWO

Machete Wounds from Paper Cuts

I still struggle when I try to explain all the variables that led to that moment. It's difficult to express the internal, accumulated pressure that led me to lock myself in my parents' bathroom with Mom's gun in my hand. Like a beach ball slowly being inflated underwater, I simply reached a tipping point after years of burying my emotions and wrestling with the thoughts their faulty, feeling-based logic produced. That day at the end of September, however, I could no longer keep the beach ball beneath the surface or prevent it from bursting at the seams.

Many of my elders, especially my parents and teachers, kept telling me these were the best years of my life, but if these were the best, I knew I'd never survive the rest of my life. Oh, I understood I was young and should feel carefree and unburdened by the adult responsibilities I'd soon encounter. But the upside to adulthood—experience, knowledge, maturity—didn't seem to offer any hope for healing or relief. I sat through my high school classes in a daze, thoroughly convinced there had to be more to life but uncertain how to open that door and walk through it.

After word spread that I'd shot myself, people in my community found it hard to understand the accumulation of pain that led to that moment. They couldn't understand why such a nice girl, one they considered so pretty and pleasant, someone who seemingly had so much to live for, wanted to end her life. Local gossip insisted there had to be some incident or traumatic event that sent me spiraling over the edge.

But there simply wasn't. By way of explanation, I now compare it to the way we dismiss paper cuts because they're such small, surface injuries that rarely bleed and quickly heal. If the paper continued to saw at the same wound over and over again, however, it would create a deep gash that could have been made by a machete. Others only saw the minor surface incidents, the paper cuts of my life, but I felt each razor-sharp moment amplified as it echoed into a much deeper chasm of pain. Perhaps sharing a few examples will give you an idea of what I'm talking about.

———

My parents divorced when I was four.

I'll never forget driving away from the house where we

had lived with a terrible sense that nothing would ever be the same. Looking out the back window of my mom's Buick sedan, I watched my father straining to hide his tears as he waved from the front porch. My oldest sister and only brother stood stiff as statues beside him on each side. The air fogged up with palpable tension, and all I remember is that weight, that dread knotting my stomach.

Something vital to us all had broken, a support beam had cracked and splintered like a tree branch unable to bear its own weight. My other sister and I rode away with Mom while the other half of us remained there in the place we had all once called home. Nothing was the way it should be.

Looking back through adult eyes, I'm surprised my parents' marriage lasted as long as it did. They had married after my mom became pregnant with my oldest sister and moved close to where my father's close-knit Syrian parents and extended family lived. While my dad's grandparents had been the first generation born in the United States, no one had married anyone without Syrian blood before my father. His mother was a gruff, no-nonsense woman with stern eyes that rarely betrayed her deep emotions. Apparently, it was clear from the start she was not pleased with my father's decision to marry my mother.

And I can just imagine how hard it must have been for Mom trying to fit in. Women were not highly esteemed in her in-laws' household, likely a remnant of their Middle Eastern culture. I remember family dinners at my grandmother's where she served elaborate, traditional Syrian dishes, beginning with balls of *shanklish* and *kibbeh*, hot *fatteh* bread dipped in olive oil, followed by lamb spiced with onions and garlic, sesame and grape leaves. The meal ended with thick, black coffee for the adults and a selection of honey-flavored sweets and sliced fruits. While the food was delicious, the undercurrent of tension between my father's parents and my mother prevented me from enjoying these exotic feasts.

My mother remained wary, guarded at those events. She had grown up in a dysfunctional family in West Texas, with a father who rejected her. Constantly feeling like an outsider had to have been so lonely and painful, stirring up toxic memories of her childhood. The fact that Mom's first child was a daughter didn't help matters. She was acutely reminded of this disappointment as if it were somehow a failure on her part.

As my father climbed the corporate ladder and traveled more frequently for work, my mother was left to perfect her household to my grandmother's standards. I suspect Mom never felt it was good enough no matter how often she dusted, vacuumed, scrubbed, and washed. An impeccable housekeeper naturally, Mom only became more critical of herself, honing a perfectionism that would put Martha Stewart to shame.

By the time I was born, the baby of the family, my parents' marriage had already started its downward spiral. Years later my father admitted that he never really loved my mother the way he knew he should have, that even though he chose to marry her and worked at loving her, his commitment never took root and blossomed into the kind of love that withstands the inevitable droughts of hardship.

———

At the time, I sensed both my father and his family blamed Mom for the divorce, as if she had done something to cause it. But none of it made sense to me. My confusion was compounded by the fact that my parents were granted split—not joint—custody of the four of us. Such a court ruling was unusual then and reflected the stubborn strength of both my parents. Dad impressed the judge with his stability, intelligence, and job as a corporate executive in El Paso. While mothers tended to be awarded custody, Mom seemed resigned to the fact that this new arrangement would have to work.

Staying with my mother meant moving back to Odessa, more than six hours east of where Dad and my two older siblings lived now. No one told me directly, but I sensed I wouldn't be seeing any of them very often. In fact, no one explained anything about the divorce to me, but then again, it probably would have been difficult because I was so young. But even as I got older, my parents rarely talked about their feelings or explained their decisions. The motives and emotions of my family members remained a potent mystery, unknown but powerful enough to create permanent damage.

A few months after the divorce was final, my mother

remarried a friend of my dad's from high school. He offered her a nice home and a solid chance at the love, acceptance, and security she had never known—either growing up or during her first marriage.

Adjusting to my stepfather confused me at first. A short period of time went by, and all I really knew was that I had a new dad, so naturally that's what I started calling him. Hearing me call him Dad just melted Bill's heart. I wasn't trying to belittle my father, and I still loved him just as much, but it just seemed natural. I assumed I now had two dads: the old one who lived with my siblings and the new one who lived with me.

My relationship with my other father, however, grew distant. He phoned occasionally but never seemed to have much time, and I didn't have much to say. But one weekend about a year after the divorce, my mom told us we were going to visit him, and I so looked forward to reconnecting with him and my brother and sister. But as I soon discovered, the connection that came so easily with Bill would not work with the woman who was soon to become my stepmother.

———

One weekend, when I was about five, I went to visit my father in El Paso, Texas, where I'd been born. Upon my arrival at his house, he explained that we were going to spend the day with a female friend of his. I didn't mind—I was just so excited to be there with my father! I had missed him and had such a void in my heart since we moved. The thought of spending time with him brought me so much joy that I couldn't quit smiling.

"Tammy, this is my friend Mary," my dad said, and I grinned up at her, unsure whether to hug her or offer my hand. "Mary, this is my baby girl, Tammy."

Unfortunately, his friend wasn't as excited to see me as I was to meet her. Before the words were out of Dad's mouth, she clearly felt ambushed and wasn't having it.

"What is *she* doing here?" Mary barked. "Have you *lost* your mind? You think I want a little kid tagging along with us today?"

"Uh, hello," I whispered, glued in place beside my father.

"Sweetie, I need to talk to Mary for a minute, okay? Why don't you color me a picture in that book you brought? We'll be right back," Dad said.

I nodded and went into the little kitchen, pulled up a chair, and began taking my crayons out of my backpack. I loved to color pictures as a child. It's become a popular adult fad now, and I understand why—the soothing, orderly motions combined with the power to choose any colors you want is quite relaxing.

While I colored Barney the purple dinosaur, my dad took his girlfriend to the other room. He was clearly trying to keep his voice down, but she would have none of it.

"I thought we were going to spend a romantic day together! Just you and me! How's that going to work with Little Orphan Annie out there looking over our shoulders, huh?"

My father said something I couldn't make out to which Mary yelled, "I don't care what you told her! Tell her something else! I really can't believe you, you know that? I thought you were really into me, but I guess not. Why else would you bring your kid along on our date?"

I felt so ashamed for being there since it was pretty obvious I wasn't wanted. As an adult I know it wasn't my fault, but at the time, I felt as if I were ruining my dad's life. After my father calmed Mary down, they walked out of the bedroom with a little baby in a carrier and all of us left. I remember riding in the back seat of the car wishing I wasn't there. I wanted to be with my father, but I knew my presence was causing him problems. I remember thinking that if I had not been there, my father and this lady with the big blonde hair and red lipstick would have been better off.

———

By my next visit the following year, I was determined to make up for getting off to such a rocky start with my father and Mary, who had just become his wife. I enjoyed such a good relationship with my stepdad, Bill, back in Odessa that I just assumed it would now be that way with my new stepmom. I tried so very hard to make her like me. I tried being really nice to her, and I did my best not to talk back or get into trouble, but no matter what I did or didn't do, it was clear how she felt. All her attention was focused on the toddler crawling around on the floor, the little boy who I discovered was my new stepbrother.

Toward the end of my visit, I had an idea: *Well, I have two dads and now I have two moms, so the right thing to do is to call my stepmom "Mom" just like I call Bill "Dad."* Boy, was I wrong!

Mary and Dad were in their bathroom getting dressed when I bounded in and said, "Good morning, Mom!"

My stepmother dropped her brush with a clatter on the vanity where she stood doing her hair in front of the mirror. "Don't you ever call me that! I am not your mother!"

Dad rushed in and said, "What's the matter?"

When she told him, he very patiently took me in his arms and tried to calm her down at the same time. But I was clearly the one causing the problem.

The rejection I kept facing with my stepmom was absolutely crushing me, and I couldn't figure out why I so disgusted her. Now I know her resentment and jealousy had nothing to do with me personally, just the role I played in my father's life. But at the time the why behind her vehemence didn't matter. The seeds of shame and insecurity were already taking root.

———

My father never totally rejected me, but my interpretation of his actions left a distinct impression. As a young child who didn't understand adult situations, I wasn't able to grasp the pressures he must have felt while trying to unite and love a blended family. Dad didn't realize I was absorbing such toxic, painful emotions because I was so determined to be a good girl and cause no further trouble. But my insecurity grew and I began to worry that others—not just my father and his new family—really didn't like having me around.

My stepmom did nothing to dispel this feeling. Whenever I went on vacation to see them, I would become physically ill from the stress of knowing that I wasn't wanted, but I couldn't do anything about it. In all fairness, I believed my father wanted me; it just appeared that he didn't have time for me. Either way, I felt rejected. He was always working or busy doing activities with the other kids, and I just happened to be there, another kid in the background. It seemed as though everything was about someone else. Children need to know they are significant and loved. But the older I got, the more I questioned my importance and my own self-worth.

By the time I entered adolescence, I mostly kept to myself and remained quiet unless with friends with whom I wanted to fit in. Then I'd plaster on a big smile, laugh a lot, and act as if I enjoyed being with them as much as I desperately wanted them to enjoy being with me. I didn't think I was fooling any of them, but they still welcomed me back most of the time.

One incident stands out: a big showdown with a pack of mean girls in middle school. These peers made an art form out of put-downs and sharp critiques of basically everyone at school. No one was immune—classmates, teachers, parents, or anyone else. While I desperately wanted to be liked and part of the in-group, I struggled to laugh at remarks I found mean, spiteful, and hurtful. Finally, the group went too far, and their antics caught the attention of several teachers and our school guidance counselor. Each young lady came before them for a conversation about their latest bullying stunt, this one involving someone with a disability.

When it was my turn, I blushed bright red from the embarrassment of the situation. I had not actively participated, but these teachers knew I sometimes hung out with these girls and wanted them to like me. After a mild scolding that nonetheless brought tears to my eyes, one teacher handed me a tissue and said, "Tamara, you're better than this. Some of these girls . . . I don't know what to say. But you have a kind heart. Don't let them get to you. Don't compromise who you are to be part of their vicious pack."

Her words sobered me, mostly because I felt as if she had looked right into my soul. Someone saw me—*the real me*. I felt I did have a kind heart—too kind, in fact. I hated to tease and be teased the way so many of my classmates enjoyed back-and-forth name calling and crude joking. And even when I knew they were teasing, I still replayed our dialogue and wondered if they really meant what they'd said—about my looks, my hair, my figure, the way I dressed, anything.

My kind heart couldn't take it.

———

Soon my daydreams became rewinds of that day's conversations. I turned words, actions, and situations over and over, and was almost always left feeling small, worthless, and unwanted. By the time I entered high school, the least little thing could set me off and make me feel like a total dunce. For example, I remember coming home from school one hot spring day and to my delight discovering that Mom had brought home a carton of Blue Bell chocolate ice cream. Mom knew it was my favorite and smiled as I dished up a scoop and offered her a bite. Instead of returning the carton to the freezer, however, I opened the fridge and placed the ice cream beside a jug of sun tea before closing the door and returning to my bowl.

"I can't believe you just did that, Tam!" Mom shrieked. "Get your head out of the clouds and pay attention! Put that ice cream back in the freezer before it melts." She didn't mean to sound harsh and probably thought nothing of it as she walked out of the kitchen. But for several days, I couldn't quit thinking about how stupid I must be to do something like that. I struggled to dismiss it as the small, insignificant moment that it was and instead added it to the growing internal dossier of all my faults and flaws.

Anyone else might have laughed at their absentmindedness and let it go. Everyone does silly things like this from time to time, yet I allowed every little mistake to beat me down. The negative seeds planted in my heart years ago began to bear their desperate fruit of fear, insecurity, and worthlessness.

I intended to harvest that fruit once and for all that fateful, last day of September.

I would taste it as a .38 bullet pierced my body.

That bitter fruit would take me to hell.

THREE

The Hell I Know

Before I could pull the trigger on the .38 pressed firmly against my chest, the gun fired. Instantly, with a piercing burn, the bullet tore through my body. Struggling to breathe as if underwater, I realized blood was flooding my lungs. It was only a matter of seconds before I would feel no more pain and see eternity. Although my goal had been accomplished, throughout this ordeal I never stopped praying for God to forgive me, crying out to Jesus because I knew he alone could save me. I knew what I was doing was wrong, and I pleaded to be forgiven with all my heart, desperate for his mercy.

Even as I sensed my soul leaving my body, I never lost awareness of what was taking place. My body crumpled to the floor of the tiled shower stall. The smell of gunpowder enveloped me. My vision dimmed and I heard the faint sounds of Foxy's barking in our backyard. Then I slipped into a silent darkness. Gasping for my last breath, I closed my eyes as my body shut down.

This was it.

I was dead.

———

Please keep in mind that throughout this experience, I was not in my physical body. I was in another realm of existence, one terrifying and unfamiliar. Though I've tried to describe what happened to me next, I know of no way to adequately articulate what I experienced. The sensation of falling consumed me, and I felt disoriented by the blackness surrounding me and the speed with which I traveled downward. I struggled to understand what was going on and to accept that I was no longer in control—someone else was.

No longer able to feel my body, I nevertheless sensed my soul hurtling through darkness, like a shadow sucked into a wind tunnel. As I left my body, I began traveling at what seemed faster than the speed of light, as my entire being plummeted deeper and darker into an unknown void. Like a jumper with no parachute or bungee cord, I was freefalling without any sense of when or even if I would land. Despite being aware I was no longer in my mortal body, I still felt both emotions and something similar to physical sensations, only more intense. I felt incredibly sensitive to my surroundings as terror swept through me, a sense of utter helplessness, as if I had jumped out of a rocket ship into endless space, falling, falling deeper into complete darkness.

Like most teenagers, I loved riding roller coasters at amusement parks and savoring the adrenaline-spiked thrill of being so high before falling so fast. But there was no excitement or anticipation of enjoyment as I raced toward infinity—only an intensity that was off the charts, as if every cell of my being, every speck of the DNA of my existence, was being reduced to fear. I knew then that God is our energy source, and that without him, I was transformed into nothing but pure torment. Just as a chemical compound can change dramatically when one element is removed, I was no longer the same self I had once been. The essence of God in me had evaporated.

As I kept falling, I knew with absolute certainty there was nothing I could do. I was no longer in control of my destiny—I had made a choice with irrevocable, permanent, eternal consequences. *What had I done?*

———

Just as quickly as I had been whisked into the darkness, I crossed an expanse, which I immediately knew to be a kind of boundary, a gulf separating this sweeping, barren space from other regions. Somehow I knew heaven must be beyond, but I had entered ultimate darkness, a darkness so black that you couldn't see an object if it were on the tip of your nose. There was absolutely no light.

This wasn't space as we think of outer space with stars and planets and galaxies. This was space in its most basic, desolate, murky form. Looking back now, I think of the way Genesis begins, "Now the earth was formless and empty, darkness was over the surface of the deep, and the Spirit of God was hovering over the waters" (Gen. 1:2). Only, the Spirit of God was most definitely not hovering over the vacant shadowy void where I had landed—he was nowhere near. It remains the loneliest, most desolate, most frightening place I've ever encountered.

As soon as I had landed in this dismal swamp of spiritual desolation, I experienced a new sensation. Droplets of what felt like acid pelted me with countless pinpricks of excruciating pain. This acid rain, as I've come to think of it, drenched my entire being both within and without. If that was not torturous enough, it seemed like a massive, high-pressured hose sprayed the acid to make sure it hit every molecule of my being. In life I had never come close to experiencing this kind of pain, and I know it's impossible to experience anything like it on earth. This was raw agony. Fire burned through me like an electric current, saturating my soul and blistering every ounce of my being. And there was nothing I could do to stop it—*nothing.*

Worst of all, I had an acute awareness that this was what I deserved. I realized I was banished completely and eternally from the presence of the one true God. If, as many scientists believe, there is an invisible binding energy within every living atom, the place where I found myself was surely characterized by its complete absence. Arriving in hell, I was now permanently separated from my Creator, the God of the universe, the source of all light and life.

I realized my soul had been transformed into a being of sin and death. I had actually become total sin, and my eyes were opened to the fact that sin is a state of being, not just an act. I became everything that God the Father is not: I was the complete opposite of God's character, I had nothing good within me, and I turned into the opposite of love, a being of total fear, absorbed by the hopelessness of despair. I became entirely absent from love.

———

Aware of my eternal fate, I screamed out into the void around me, suddenly aware of the countless souls around me also screaming, howling, and crying out in agony. Hot scorching winds amplified the anguish in a shrieking chorus of pain. Screams crashed like horrendous waves from all those surrounding me. A stench like burning flesh, rotten eggs, and raw sewage smothered us, emanating from the essence of this place. With my senses heightened, I burned in raw agony, inhaling this atrocious sulfuric odor.

Wrenching loneliness consumed me as I looked across the fiery pit and saw innumerable souls just like me, each one contorted by pain. Each distinct being was begging for another chance, yet we all knew such relief was not only unlikely—it was simply impossible. Although we seemed right next to one another, we could not communicate or touch.

Nonetheless, I peered into each being and immediately knew everything, and I mean, *everything*—talk about too much information—about each soul. I knew each one's complete story: their life's events, actions, emotions, families, choices, sins, addictions, shame, guilt, and how they died prior to arriving in our shared prison of pure pain. My vision scrolled through each person as if viewing an old-time movie reel, seeing image after image, frame after frame, of their entire lives. We were together yet in total isolation from one another, a collective of tormented, disconnected individual souls.

There were no secrets. As I looked at any particular person, I knew everything—not one sin or action was hidden. I knew his or her family lineage, background, everything this person had ever done wrong, every sin committed, and all the sorrow the person had experienced.

The others also knew everything about me—every boy I'd kissed, every test I'd cheated on, every lie I'd told, every sin I had ever committed. Every selfish act or secret shameful thought was out there for all to see and know. Complete transparency of minds, emotions, and wills revealed each of our lives from beginning to the end. Our souls were now laid bare, and we no longer had physical bodies to clothe and disguise our spirits.

We were totally alone and totally vulnerable.

There was nowhere to hide.

No escape.

———

In the midst of our overwhelming awareness of one another, there was an even greater realization demanding our attention, a spiritual revelation of ultimate reality. My knowledge was made perfect. Revelation of truth and pure wisdom became a part of me. I no longer had questions because infinite knowledge of life, creation, God, and all of existence down to the last detail was known to all. Yet the only information of significance was the awareness that Jesus Christ, God's only Son, is Lord for eternity. Truly nothing else matters, and we all knew that *it is all about him.* We understood that the purpose of life itself is to bring honor and glory to Jesus Christ. That's the meaning of life—it was that simple!

As I looked into the eyes of each separate soul around me, I saw my own devastating sorrow mirrored back. Looking from one then to another even as they saw into me, we each understood we had lived our mortal lives blind to the fact that Jesus Christ is the true living God and there were no other gods before him. Nothing in any human heart should take his rightful place. Nothing else could give the eternal life he gives.

We knew we were in this place because we foolishly ignored God, his Word, and the truth about our desperate need for the Savior, Jesus Christ. Regardless of the circumstances of our lives or the many other people we might blame, the consequence of our decision, whether made deliberately or by default, was eternal.

We no longer had hope in any form.

Lack of hope is the very essence of hell.

Our pain would never cease.

———

Despite our inability to communicate, we all knew in some mutually intuitive way that none of us wanted anyone still alive on earth to endure the grueling anguish we were suffering there in hell. Any one of us would have been willing to continue enduring our pain if somehow we could communicate with our loved ones and prevent them from ever joining us in such despair.

As I became more acclimated to my surroundings in this surreal, supernatural place, I perceived many different chambers around me despite the darkness. Without seeing specifically who and what was in each chamber, I was aware in the fullness of my spiritual knowledge that these caverns were designed to be more torturously agonizing for certain individuals. Much later I would find references and descriptions in the Bible's book of Revelation that reflect my glimpses of these chambers.

As much as I want to describe what I perceived there, I can't even come close to the actuality of such terrifying evil. I share all this not to scare you, entertain you, or convince you. I share my experience of hell merely to warn you.

———

While my mobility was limited, I also became aware of some kind of giant creature behind me. Because I could not perceive this creature directly, it remains truly indescribable. But the ferocious fear emanating from its body, the sulfuric stench radiating from its breath upon me, the penetrating gaze of its many eyes from multiple heads—these details are forever seared into my consciousness. I'm tempted to compare this creature to a dragon, but such a comparison falls far short of the terror inspired by this demonic entity's presence. However, this was not Satan.

I was only allowed to snatch a glimpse of him, and for that I am grateful—no eyes have ever seen a more terrifying sight. Although I could scarcely see him, I could feel a presence made up of intense and violent fear. There was so much more I wasn't allowed to look upon. No words in the human vocabulary could possibly describe the hell I was in, like a place the Bible describes as Gehenna (Jer. 7:31; 19:2–6), a valley of ashes from sacrificial deaths, a trash heap of wasted lives and smoldering despair.

As unbelievable or even ludicrous as it may sound to you, I was dead—and I was in hell. I had become nothing but a tormented soul who consisted of everything as hideous as anything you can imagine. No scary movie, science fiction dreamscape, or horror novel compares to this experience that I assumed was my fate for all eternity. Loneliness was no longer in me; it simply was the essence of my being.

Fear and a comprehensive awareness of evil—that is, the complete absence of God and his goodness—pervaded and saturated my spirit. I was utterly and absolutely alone.

Coming to terms with this new and permanent reality, I tried to cry out. My futile screams continued as I called out into the darkness, desperately begging for relief, for help, for hope, for another chance. Time had ceased to exist, but I felt as if I'd been there in my torment for my entire existence.

Then I suddenly realized a kind of horizon looming above and beyond the shores of the fiery lake simmering before me and the many other souls in hell. My wailing never stopped as I looked out across the vast expanse and saw all three realms with a kind of radiant light faintly glowing at an infinite distance away. Each was separated from the other by what appeared to be a massive river or channel of water, although there was no current flowing. Without any basis of reference, I knew I was glimpsing heaven, which made my awareness of my separation from it even harsher.

Between the fiery shores of damnation where I now existed and the three realms of heaven emerging, I also saw what appeared to be our universe in its entirety. We think it is so large, which it is by our human standards, but our universe is actually very small compared to the other areas of existence. There was also a great gulf separating the heavens and the vast deep that has no end. As I looked upon our universe and saw what we call earth, it was magnified as if enlarged through a telescope. So small and so distant. So far removed from the reality I was now doomed to experience.

Suddenly, I was aware of a mighty cloud rushing toward me, something as fresh and cool as a mountain breeze, yet something I couldn't feel or experience but just simply knew was moving in my direction. Somehow the darkness around me began to dissipate as light infused the perimeter of the spot where my soul had been staked. As the wind became stronger, I looked up to see what I knew to be the Spirit of God, a cloud-like presence, and as the light became brighter, I realized it was coming directly for me.

The Spirit reached a point where he didn't need to go any farther. Thoughts raced through me as I thought of all the people on earth, living their lives like nothing mattered, who would one day be in the same place where I was standing unless they learned the truth of God and accepted the free gift of salvation through his Son, Jesus. Just as I had been doing only moments ago, a lifetime ago, people were going to work and to school, to home and even to church, ignorant of their true purpose and oblivious to the spiritual reality of their existence. I so desperately wanted them to know and more importantly to act on this severe knowledge.

The white cloud of the Holy Spirit came closer then, hovering but only reaching out for one. As he came closer still, I experienced an enormous hand of divine light and life reaching for me. Without a doubt, I knew it was the hand of God.

And he was reaching for me.

For me!

FOUR

Heaven Can't Wait

If hell is difficult to describe, heaven is utterly indescribable.

Heaven is better than anything you can imagine. Better than basking in the sun on the beaches of a tropical paradise. Better than the endorphin rush of your hardest workout. Better than the warm embrace of the person you love most. Better than enjoying a private concert in the home of your favorite singer. Better than the taste of chocolate chip cookies hot out of the oven.

Heaven is simply *better than* anything you've experienced and everything you can imagine. Looking back and trying to describe heaven, I'm reminded of what the Bible tells us, "No eye has seen, no ear has heard, and no mind has imagined what God has prepared for those who love him" (1 Cor. 2:9 NLT).

When I try to describe my visit to hell and then to

heaven, words are inadequate. Nonetheless, I'll do my best to share what this indescribable experience was like for me. Part of the problem is simply the limitations of language and human vocabulary. Any spiritual experience is difficult to describe, but sometimes I believe heaven is harder to describe—and more difficult for others to grasp—than hell.

Virtually everyone experiences pain in this life, whether it's physical suffering, mental illness, or emotional anguish, however, there is no comparison to hell's reality. Nor is there a basis of comparison that would help us comprehend the glory that is heaven, the dwelling place of God and the eternal home for those who know him through his Son, Jesus Christ.

Heaven often gets depicted as a place in the clouds where angels play harps inside the pearly gates along streets of gold. That was not my experience any more than a cartoon version of flames and pitchforks when I was in hell. Perhaps my visit to heaven stands out more because it contrasted so dramatically with the torment I had just left behind. After hearing of my description of heaven, many people tell me it reminds them of something they've seen in a movie or read in a book or heard from someone else's experience. While they may find similarities, I have deliberately avoided reading the accounts of other people with stories similar to my own, or hearing the way others describe heaven. I don't want to dilute the vivid memory I have of my experience, and I also don't want to be unintentionally influenced by others' depictions and experiences.

My visit to heaven remains a longing in my heart. I can't

wait to return home to God's presence. Heaven is more than real—it is the ultimate reality.

———

While I languished in the misery of hell, I could see an intense, immense brightness emanating from the other side of the vast expanse, the great gulf separating where I was from what was beyond. I saw the earth almost as if through a telescope or giant magnifying glass, and the entire universe within infinite space. Yet somehow beyond it all, an energetic light vibrated at the edge of it. And without a doubt, I knew that this white, shimmering place was the dwelling of the Most High, the place we usually refer to as heaven.

Even as I sensed this place from which I was cut off, I continued to cry out, "Forgive me, Lord! Please forgive me!" And in the depths of my being, I begged, "Lord, please send someone back to tell everyone the truth! Please show them your truth and your mercy!"

I longed for the fog, the boundary, the barrier, the veil to be removed from all the people I loved who were living their lives back on earth. I didn't want them—or anyone—to experience the excruciating, relentless torture of utter separation from God that I was now experiencing in death. I wanted the Lord, in his mercy, to open their eyes so they might be spared eternal torment. I wanted everyone to know the truth and to be set free by the mercy of God and the power of his Spirit.

While still crying out for God's mercy, I witnessed a cloud moving toward me, stretching itself into a form resembling a giant hand, scooping me up and transporting me toward the brightness from which it came. Immediately, I felt the lack within my soul vanish as the fullness of being with God infused me. In an instant I became whole, joined and merged in unity and oneness with God's Spirit. While linear time as we know it didn't exist, in one moment I was trapped in the despair of hell—and then in the twinkling of an eye, I had not only escaped the pain of hell but I'd been filled with the complete balm of healing, forgiveness, and wholeness.

It was like being part of a puzzle separated from the whole and suddenly fitting back into the wholeness to which I belonged. While time did not exist, even as I experienced this completion, I was travelling rapidly over the great gulf separating hell from heaven, approaching the boundary of this bright realm. While I did not enter through a gate of any kind, I nonetheless found myself immersed in the new and vast terrain of this ethereal realm.

Simply put, I was home.

I was home in the truest sense of that sensation we all want, that feeling of belonging and acceptance. It wasn't just the sense that I belonged there—*it was the knowledge that I was created for this place, to be united with my Creator.* Since then, I believe this is how Adam and Eve felt as they experienced oneness with God in the garden of Eden prior to their sinful disobedience.

At once, the colors shimmered with life, so vivid and

saturated with a vitality unlike anything I had ever encountered before. The only thing I can compare these intense, transparent colors to is the northern lights, also known as the aurora borealis, the shifting electrically charged collision of particles from the sun entering earth's atmosphere near its polar regions. This phenomenon causes the night skies to be drenched with moving colors, usually a mesmerizing blend of greens and blues, often infused with hints of pink and yellow.

But heaven radiated with an even more intense spectrum of colors.

This hyper-rainbow effect showered the terrain in this realm with energy. I say terrain because I don't know what else to call it—similar to a kind of landscape with rocks and lush foliage, only not like anything human eyes have ever seen. In fact, I was not allowed to "see" anything in detail in the way we usually think of our eyes working. I simply knew where I was as I absorbed knowledge of its environment. For instance, I knew the rocks themselves were alive and living just as plants on earth are living organisms. Yet I didn't have to directly gaze upon them to know they were present and alive. Now part of this new setting, I breathed in life itself, the sheer energy of God's presence.

Consumed by unconditional love, I knew this was the place where we all desire to go when we leave our physical bodies on earth, the place we're made for and the place we inherently crave, the place where we dwell with God. I was both humbled and exhilarated at once, aware of being in the habitat of love in its purest form, the holy place of divine perfection. I was in the presence of the one and only living God, my heavenly Father and Creator of all that exists.

Our mortal dreams simply cannot grasp the awe-inspiring reality of such eternal peace, joy, and beauty. My pain and suffering departed completely, as if I had never experienced them at all, and I felt whole and complete, washed clean and made pure throughout my being. Such glory is too exquisite for words, but I'm often reminded of the words of the psalmist:

> How lovely is your dwelling place,
>> LORD Almighty!
> My soul yearns, even faints,
>> for the courts of the LORD;
> my heart and my flesh cry out
>> for the living God.
> Even the sparrow has found a home,
>> and the swallow a nest for herself,
>> where she may have her young—
> a place near your altar,
>> LORD Almighty, my King and my God.
> Blessed are those who dwell in your house;
>> they are ever praising you.
>
> (Ps. 84:1–4)

I continued passing through heaven, almost as if flying through its atmosphere, gently gliding above its terrain, but not with angel's wings or any kind of propulsion. The sensation was like hang-gliding with my eyes closed, moving at what seemed faster than the speed of light but without the sense of adrenaline-induced excitement such an activity produces on earth. It's the sense of movement and an awareness of the surrounding environment a baby might have while being carried by a parent—protected and safe, yet knowing there is so much more beyond.

In addition to the saturated hues of color, I smelled a faint scent that only enhanced my utter enjoyment of this place, the epitome of beauty. Like everything else, it defies description, but it reminded me of the gentle fragrance of roses after a spring shower, a light perfume of perfection, perhaps the distillation of the very essence of life itself. I have never smelled anything like it since then and know I won't again until I return there to dwell forever.

Throughout this sojourn, I was not allowed to see anyone but was nonetheless aware of the presence of others. Whether there were familiar faces or other loved ones, I couldn't be sure. I simply knew I was not the only one present before God in his glory, and I wasn't allowed to know any more. I understood my restrictions were coming from God. While I knew Jesus was there with me in the fullness of God's Trinity of Father, Son, and Spirit, I did not encounter Christ directly. This didn't disappoint me or concern me because I was too fulfilled by my awareness of God's presence. I desired only to worship him in all the fullness of his complete glory.

I neither needed nor wanted anything else.

Only God.

Even as I experienced such full joy of God's presence and felt his sacred energy infuse my being, I knew that I was only passing through this place. The choice was not mine. Again, I was simply aware that it was not the appointed time for me to remain in this place that would be the ultimate home for my soul. I was there just to visit, to experience firsthand the completeness of being with God, utterly whole, entirely forgiven and washed clean of my sin nature.

Then, sensing my movement back into the dark expanse I had passed over to arrive there, I began to leave heaven. I was not backtracking the same route by which I had departed from hell and entered heaven but instead crossed over the infinite space until I approached the universe and saw the sphere of the earth, like a blue and green marble far away. Then suddenly I was entering Earth's atmosphere, aware that I was returning from the spiritual journey that had transformed every aspect of my being for eternity. I continued descending, back toward my house there in West Texas, passing through its shingled roof as if walking into a light wind. I then found myself back in my body, aware of the painful hole in my chest and the enormous amount of blood pooling around me on the tiles of my mother's bathroom.

I was alive again.

I opened my eyes, vaguely aware of a fluttering above me as I sensed the fullness of the Lord's presence leaving my soul. I could also see and hear my surroundings again, although I remained disoriented by the sharp contrast between the spiritual journey I had just experienced and the confinement of being back in my teenage body. Despite the pain in my chest, I realized that only a few minutes prior, before the gun went off in my hand and the bullet entered my body, I had felt totally hopeless with no desire to live. Now, though, I was not only alive but had a passionate desire to live.

More than just my physical and emotional state had been altered. I was keenly aware that I had now been born again, saved by the blood of Jesus on the cross, a new creature in Christ. I was radically different from the girl I had been only minutes before—not because of my out-of-body, otherworldly experiences but because Jesus was in my heart and God's Spirit was living in me.

I was filled with hope, aware that with Jesus in my life I could face anything that came my way. I was also aware of my mission and newfound purpose. My responsibility was to tell people about the reality of hell and the awe-inspiring wonder of heaven. This experience convinced me that everyone needs to know how much God loves and cares about us, how much he longs for us to be in relationship with him and to know him. How he wants us all to come home to him one day after our lives on earth are completed.

Let me say it again: heaven and hell are real—*heaven and hell are spiritual realities.*

FIVE

Back to Life

"Mom? Mom—I need you . . ."

I struggled to breathe. Back in my body after my surreal spiritual journey, I labored with each breath. Something heavy was squeezing my lungs, and I felt like I was under water. I could hear my mother walking through the living room and remembered she had been in the backyard gardening. Foxy yapped at the door wanting to follow her in.

"Mom!" I called out again.

"Tam? Where are you?"

"In . . . in your bathroom." I could barely get the words out because my throat closed like a fist each time I tried to speak. Blood continued to seep steadily from my chest. I felt so bad for making such a mess in Mom's immaculate bathroom. What would I tell her? How could I ever explain what had just happened to me in the previous minutes here on earth?

"What are you doing in there?" She jiggled the door handle. "It's locked—are you okay?"

"You need to call an ambulance," I said as calmly as possible. "I shot myself."

Silence for a beat, just a half second.

"You *what*?" Her voice rose an octave as she processed the news I'd just shared. "Oh my God, Tam, what happened?"

Mom frantically shook the door, trying to force the lock. She pounded her fists and then dashed away, and I could hear her talking on the phone to the 9-1-1 operator. She sounded hysterical, swallowing tears so she could share our address. "Hurry, dear Lord, *please hurry!*" she shrieked. Then I heard her footsteps charge out the door from the kitchen into the garage.

"Mom?" I called out again, trying to shift my weight away from the side of my body where the bullet had passed. What was she doing now? Then her footfalls beat a rhythm toward me again.

Boom! Boom! Boom! Back at the locked bathroom door separating us, my mother pounded the lock with a sledgehammer until it gave. "Oh, my baby!" she whispered.

I must have been a sight for her to behold. Crumpled into a heap on the floor of the shower stall, bright red smeared all over the white tiles, and a gun in my hand. In that moment I would have done anything to spare my mother the sight of her baby girl in such shape.

My mother stood by me and kept talking softly. I couldn't make out her words, but just the sound of her voice soothed me. I wanted to speak to her but couldn't muster the energy.

A siren wailed toward us, and Mom rushed to the front door. I heard unfamiliar voices, at least two, and then it seemed like a crowd of people suddenly filled the small room with me. They knelt beside me, one taking my pulse and the other gently sliding the gun away.

"It's faint but there's a pulse," a man said. "Get that gurney in here!"

"What's her name?" he asked, and I heard my mother say, "Tammy—Tamara."

"Tammy," another one said, a woman with short, dark hair. "Can you hear me?"

"Yes," I managed. My voice worked but my throat felt so dry.

The female EMT cradled the side of my head with her hand and with the other shined a bright penlight in my eyes. For a moment the bright light made me wish I was returning to the radiant glow of heaven, but then I felt something being placed on my chest, over the bullet hole, and I knew I was definitely back in my body. I felt unusually alert but also very calm.

"On three," said the man, counting, "one, two, three," and then pairs of hands lifted my body and unfolded me onto the gurney jutting into the doorway. I felt the bumps and heard the rattles as they wheeled me out our front door, down the porch, across the driveway, and toward the back end of the ambulance. With both its rear doors flung open, it looked like the mouth of a giant monster waiting to eat me. My soul shivered then, recalling the horrors I had witnessed in hell only moments ago.

Then we stopped as my mother reached for my hand. "She's so pale!" she said, crying. "Please don't let her die! Please save her—please!"

"Mom, everything is going to be all right," I said, opening my eyes as fully as possible. "I'm okay."

She cried out, "Oh, baby, you are not okay—you're dying!"

"If we're going to bother to go, then we need to go now!" one of the paramedics barked. My mother nodded and stepped back as two other EMTs lifted me into the mouth of the giant.

I hated for her to worry but didn't know how to reassure her. I knew I must look like death warmed over, as my grandmother liked to say, but I still had the peace of the Lord inside me. I had already died and faced all that I could possibly face.

God had restored me to life again, so I knew he had a purpose for me. I knew I was going to be just fine. No one knew I had been to hell—and heaven—and back. I had been given a second chance at life. More important, I had been given a second chance at heaven. The next time I'd die, whenever that might be, I'd have no doubt about where I would spend eternity. Jesus was my Savior and lived in me now.

The next time I went to heaven, I would be home for eternity.

———

An engine roared, and, at the edge of my vision, I saw my stepdad's sedan squeal to a stop at the curb. His voice thundered across the driveway as my mom rushed into his arms while at the same time trying to tell him what had happened. Foxy was barking as clouds unraveled in white threads in the blue sky above me. Had I really gone to school that day? Was it only an hour ago when Mom picked me up? That all felt like *years* ago. So much had changed since then.

Dad said something to one of the paramedics who responded with authority. I could only make out his final words, "Sir, we *must* get going if we're going! Every minute still counts." They must have thought I was going to die. But I knew I wasn't. No matter how bad I may have looked, or how weak my pulse might have been, or how gray the pallor of my skin, I knew I was back. *I was alive.*

"It's not too late? *Go!* Please go!" My dad started crying then as two paramedics shut the doors of the ambulance. An IV suddenly extended from my arm, and an oxygen mask covered my mouth. I heard low voices mixed with static from the crackle of a radio set against the melody of the siren. Pain ricocheted throughout my rib cage as I tried to cough. Each bump and turn sent another horrendous jolt to my spine.

We slowed, and I could tell we'd arrived at the hospital.

"Yes, she made it," I overheard one of the EMTs tell a nurse as they extracted me from the ambulance.

They rolled me through the sliding glass doors and into the fluorescent tunnels of the hospital hallways. We landed in a room that looked like the inside of a spaceship with all its panels, knobs, and controls. I was lifted onto an exam table, amazed at the tight synchronicity of the medical team in action. "Ow!" I yelled as one of them pierced between my ribs with a surgical knife, which was immediately replaced with a tube that began draining blood away from my left lung.

Once the blood was drained, I could breathe easier, so they propped me into position for X-rays. The outline of my body appeared in shades of gray on a monitor, with my bones appearing darker from their density. The bullet had shredded its way through me, leaving many tiny fragments in its wake, but with most of it exiting out my back.

"Look," I heard one of the medics say, pointing to the screen.

"It barely missed her heart," another said. "Another quarter inch and there's no way she'd be here right now."

———

I dozed in and out of consciousness then as fluids and antibiotics coursed through my body thanks to the IV, my new best friend. Nurses, doctors, technicians, and medical assistants shuffled in and out of my room, checking my heart rate and pulse, making notes on a clipboard at the foot of my bed. Bits and pieces of their conversations buzzed in my head like the sound bites you hear while flipping channels.

"Can you believe that bullet didn't explode her heart?" a female voice with a thick Texas accent said.

"It's a miracle she's here," said another.

"Did she really pull the trigger herself?" said a male voice this time.

"That's what I heard."

"Poor thing—here, she needs two more pints."

"Honey, with a body like hers there's no reason to use a gun. She needs to learn to use what's she got to get whatever she wants." Nurse Lone Star again.

"Shoot, if I looked like her, there's nothing I couldn't have!"

Laughter echoed out the door into the hallway.

Another male voice, "If I could have a piece of that— mmm, makes my life better just thinkin' about it!"

"Quit bein' a male pig," a woman said in an angry voice as she entered the room. "Don't make me write you up. We clear?"

"Yes, doctor," the playboy said. "Didn't mean nothin' by it. She's just a pretty gal, that's all."

"Get out of here now—both of you."

I wasn't sure whether to be flattered, amused, or mad. There I was virtually naked with tubes and monitors every-where, apparently getting a transfusion to replace all the blood I lost, while members of my medical team made suggestive comments. It wasn't the safest feeling in the world, but I guess I shouldn't expect everyone else to be different just because my life had been changed forever.

I didn't hold it against them, though.

I just wanted them to know what really matters. I wanted them to know the truth of Jesus before it was too late.

——

I heard familiar voices whispering. At first I thought I must be dreaming, but then I realized my family must be in my hospital room. After my initial assessment I had been taken to the intensive care unit for recovery; but after I remained stable, I was quickly moved to a regular patient room. I had no idea what time it was or even what day it was.

The voices murmured again. I kept my eyes closed because it was too much effort to open them, let alone try to talk with my loved ones. And what would I tell them? What could I tell them? As joyful and hopeful as I felt because of the gift I had received, I wasn't sure I was prepared to deal with the fallout from what I had done.

"She looks so peaceful. I hope she's resting." I sniffed my mother's perfume faintly, a welcome floral scent instead of the antiseptic smell of the hospital.

"I just don't understand," my dad was saying. His voice sounded heavy and tired, and I wondered how long I had been there. "It's not like her."

"Something must've happened," my oldest sister said. "Tam's always been so happy, so easygoing. This isn't like her at all. So, yeah, I don't know what it was, but something happened."

"She has seemed a little down lately," Mom said. "I . . . I try to be there for her, but I can't read her mind." She began crying and I didn't know if I could bear it. "I just love her so much."

"She knows that," Dad said. "She knows how much we all love her." He swallowed hard and held back his own tears. "And the good news is she's alive. Doc said a full recovery. After her ribs heal and that hole heals up, she'll be fine."

"Unless . . . nothing," my sister started but didn't finish her thought. "Yeah, we're here for her. Tamara will be fine."

Unless she's crazy or something, I thought, finishing her sentence for her. I lay there and let their voices drift away as I dozed. Of course they were all in shock. I had told no one about how depressed I'd been feeling. And it would be hard to make them understand that nothing had happened that day to tip me over the edge. I just couldn't stand the pain anymore.

The Tammy they knew was outgoing and upbeat, fun-loving and happy-go-lucky. The daughter and sister they knew wasn't even capable of such a drastic action. They truly had no idea how deeply I felt everything in my life, from the tone of someone's voice to the pure gold color of the sunset over the West Texas horizon. And maybe I had myself to blame because I didn't let them see that side of me, the real me, the me who hurt so much for so long that she decided she'd rather die than go on living with such pain.

Yet now the most amazing, unexpected, life-changing thing had happened. I had experienced the unbearable torments of hell and been consumed by the deepest regret possible, the regret of not knowing, loving, and serving God with this precious gift of life that he gave me. And then, miraculously, the Lord had heard my prayers and shown his divine mercy on me. He loved me enough to grant my prayer and to lift me out of eternal anguish. He transported me across the dark expanse into the light of his love. God allowed me to experience wholeness with him, a taste of my heavenly home, before returning me to my body and, literally, new life.

The challenge now would be learning how to fulfill my new mission. I would have to expect others not to understand—maybe no one could, completely, except for God. I could just imagine what it would be like when I saw my friends and went back to school. It made my heart shudder just to think about how awkward that would be for a while. Yes, I knew that Jesus would be with me and that I now had a way to tell others the truth about God and what happens after you die. But still, it wasn't going to be easy.

In fact, I had no idea just how hard my life was about to become.

I had been given new life—a second chance at heaven.

But as I would soon find out, the Enemy of my soul, the evil one, would do everything in his power to discredit me and derail my mission.

SIX

Width of a Shadow

I opened my eyes and saw a familiar stranger sitting next to my hospital bed, staring intently. He was the attending doctor who had been assigned to me when I was first brought in. With dark hair peppered by silver at his temples and wire-framed glasses, he looked more like a professor than a doctor. He had especially kind eyes.

"How do you feel, Tamara?" he said and tried to smile.

I swallowed and tried to speak, but my mouth was too dry. The doctor reached for the water glass on the nearby nightstand and held it for me while I sipped from a straw. The cold water tasted so good, and I could feel it all the way down into my aching body.

"Okay," I said. "Hurts."

"Yes, you'll be in pain for a few days as your body recovers," he said, taking the water from me. "But you're very lucky to be alive." The doctor stood and retrieved the clipboard dangling from the foot of my bed. "You know that, don't you?"

I nodded as a spasm of pain raced from my chest down into my legs.

"It's really a miracle, actually. I mean, there's no medical reason why you should be alive. That bullet missed hitting your heart by no more than the width of a shadow." He scribbled something onto the chart and put it back where it had been. "I'm not a religious man, but seeing you come through this almost makes me want to believe in God." He attempted another smile. "If the pain gets too much, ring the nurse. I'll make sure you have medication available if it gets too intense. I'll be back to check on you tomorrow, okay?"

I nodded again and smiled back at him, my eyes following him out of the room. I had no idea whether it was day or night. Without windows, the fluorescent lights in my hospital room cast a dull, bluish glare that made it impossible to tell. The scent of roses and other flowers hit my nose, and I looked around at several vases of flowers, along with a teddy bear anchoring two balloons—one read "Get" and the other "Well." An oversize card with a similar message was propped next to the small TV on a shelf in the corner.

So many expressions of caring and concern filled my hospital room, but they didn't mean much to me. I appreciated the gestures, of course, and the good intentions that accompanied them, but somehow they felt hollow. The family and friends who had sent them, who apparently wanted to be there for me now during my recovery, seemed just as distant as they had the day before when I had shot myself. I assumed they didn't really want to know what happened or why I did what I did. And they certainly couldn't handle the truth of my spiritual journey to hell and heaven—not yet, anyway.

I was grateful to be alive, and the peace of being in God's presence lingered in my spirit. But coming back to the life I had so desperately wanted to escape only twenty-four hours ago was not going to be easy. I knew I was not who I had been then and that I was forever changed. But everything and everyone else seemed the same. If they couldn't understand me before my encounter with God, how would they ever accept me now?

———

The bustle of voices and increased frequency of nurses in my room signaled that it must be daytime. I hadn't been offered real food yet, but a sweet older nurse had brought me a Sprite and promised me applesauce before she finished her shift. While my body still ached, I was already growing impatient with being in the hospital. At the same time, I couldn't imagine going home and the awkward transition back to some kind of normal.

When my father, not my stepfather whom I called Dad, entered my room later that afternoon, however, he offered for me to come home with him. It would mean leaving my mom and dad there in Odessa, along with my friends at school. It would be starting over, which would be hard in some ways. But I would also have the advantage of a clean slate—no one would know what I had done. No one would be giving me funny looks and whispering about the girl who was "emotionally disturbed" and had tried to kill herself.

"Just think about it, Tam," my father said. He looked exhausted, with dark circles under his eyes and new creases on his forehead. When he'd heard the news, he had booked the first flight that morning. He clearly wanted to do whatever he could for me. His eyes brimmed with tears when he saw me, and he held my hand for the longest time. It was probably the most undivided attention I had ever had from him in my life. I could smell the scent of his cologne, a blend of spices and leather.

"Thanks, Dad," I said, my voice a raw whisper. "Let me think about it. I . . . I don't know what Mom would think."

"I'll talk to her," he said. "She will agree to whatever is best for you. You can have your own room, and you've always liked visiting, haven't you?"

I offered a weak smile, not wanting to share the painful memories I had of my sporadic trips to see him in El Paso. The harsh, unkind words from his wife and her attitude of resentment at my presence. His preoccupation with his work and long absences. Without realizing it, my father had inadvertently reminded me why I would never want to live with him and my stepmom. But I didn't have the strength to talk about it anymore.

"So tired," I said and closed my eyes.

"Of course you are," he said, patting my hand. "Get some rest. I'll be here when you wake up. Just think about my offer. We'd love to have you."

I nodded without opening my eyes, grateful to drift off once again.

———

When I woke, it seemed a crowd had gathered to watch me sleep. There were more flowers, more cards, more stuffed animals. My mom, stepdad, and several friends from school, both girls and guys, whispered among themselves, the sound like bees buzzing, until one of them looked over and blurted, "She's awake!" Everyone laughed, including me, although it hurt my chest worse than anything.

Mom raised me to a sitting position and propped another pillow behind my back. Two of my girlfriends gathered on each side of my bed like bookends, both talking at once, asking how I was doing, before pausing awkwardly. It wasn't like they could ask the questions I knew they were burning to know:

What happened?
Why did you do it?
What sent you over the edge?
How did you survive?
Will you really be okay?

I had many of the same questions myself.

Then one began playing with my hair while the other began telling me what I had missed in school that day along with well wishes from our other mutual friends. Another girl and two guys stayed by the door, and one of the guys, Kyle, met my eyes when I glanced over at him and smiled. It was a nice smile. I thought he was on the football team but couldn't remember. I didn't know him very well and figured he had just come along to satisfy his curiosity, a visit to see the girl who had shot herself and survived, like the freak show at the summer carnival.

It didn't take long before my mother politely shooed them all out, but not before they took my hand and said, "Get well soon! Love ya, Tam! We'll be back tomorrow!" I thanked them for coming and reached for a drink of water. While it was good to see them, it was also exhausting.

Again, nothing had changed. Staying on the surface of things and keeping it all superficial always exhausted me. Did they really care about me? Could they handle all that swirled inside me? I wondered how many would remain true friends in the days and weeks to come. Visiting someone in the hospital is easy; being there and caring, *really* caring, day in and day out is much harder.

"I need to run home and clean up, okay?" my mom said. "Bill will stay with you. And I'll be back tonight. Let me know if you think of anything you want me to bring you." She squeezed my hand gently and I nodded. Then I closed my eyes as she shut the door behind her.

After dozing a few minutes, I looked up and Dad was standing by my bed with a gift bag in his hands, bright tissue billowing from the top. "I brought you something," he said, placing it in my hands. I leaned forward and propped myself into a sitting position.

"You didn't have to get me anything, Dad," I said, smiling at this thoughtfulness nonetheless. "If I can just get through all this tissue paper . . ."

"Here, I'll help you," he said. He placed a rectangle into my hands. It was a framed print of the famous "Footprints" poem, about how Jesus carries us when we can't keep going.

Emotion flooded through me and tears spilled down my cheeks. Dad was not a religious man, and I was touched by his gift. He became emotional, too, as I thanked him and squeezed his hand. "It's perfect," I said.

"Don't tell your mom," he said with tears in his eyes. "But I gave my heart to Jesus yesterday. I . . . I don't know if your mom will understand, and I'm not sure how to explain it. But I want us all to start going to church together, okay?"

I nodded, speechless, letting the news sink in and praying silently in gratitude.

"Do you know which church you want to go to?" he said, wiping tears away.

I chuckled. "As a matter of fact, I saw a church . . . sort of like a round rock on top of a hill, kind of like a lighthouse."

"Hmm," he said. "Not sure I know that one but I'll find it. Once you're home I'll take you there, okay?"

I nodded again, marveling at the way God was already

working in my dad's life. I knew better than perhaps anyone about the power of Jesus to restore you when you couldn't keep going. I had experienced it firsthand in the most dramatic, life-changing way possible.

"I'm here for you, Tam," he said, choking up. "I don't know what happened yesterday, but we'll do whatever we have to do to get you well, okay? I just love you so much." He leaned in and kissed my forehead before hurrying out of the room.

I read through "Footprints" again and thought about the journey from which I had just returned. Jesus had indeed carried me when I was powerless to move on my own. Bill had no idea how much his gift meant to me. Even to this day, I keep it where I can see it regularly, a reminder of all I have been through and the faithfulness of God each step of the way.

———

When my mom returned to my bedside that evening, she said, "I told your father he didn't need to stay." I immediately knew she was referring to my biological father, not Bill. She continued, "I hope that's okay. I mean, there's really nothing he could do. I'm here. Your dad is here. We'll take care of anything you need."

"So he left already?" I asked.

She nodded. "Said he'd call and check on you tomorrow. Said he'd come back next week or any time you want him to. He also said he wanted you to come and live with him. Made it sound like that's what you wanted."

"No," I said, "he offered but I didn't say I'd go. I told him I'd think about it."

"I'm not sure that's a good idea," she said. "You need to be here at home with the people who love you most."

Thoughts and jumbled memories cascaded like a waterfall. I wanted to tell her everything right then. The same way, as a little girl, I couldn't wait to tell her all about my first day at school. But I didn't know where to begin. How do you tell your momma that you wanted to kill yourself? And that while you were dead, you experienced the excruciating torments of hell before being lifted into the glory of God's presence in the hyper-color beauty of heaven?

"It's okay, honey," she said, and pushed a strand of honey-colored hair away from my face. "You just rest, okay? You don't belong with your father—you belong here. It's all going to be fine. Doctor said you will be able to come home soon—maybe even by tomorrow if you keep getting better."

I nodded, overcome by fatigue once again. I feared that if I tried to tell her—or anyone—what I had experienced they would assume I was hallucinating or dreaming because of the heavy pain medication and all I'd been through. But I didn't doubt for a moment the intense reality I had experienced. I knew exactly what had happened. And when I told others about it, I didn't want them to have any excuses for not believing me.

———

After you try to take your own life, most people assume you're either mentally ill or you're doing it for attention. I was neither of these, but simply emotionally crushed to the point of brokenness. I wanted a life without continual, 24-7, every-minute heartache, a life without the sense of aloneness that made me feel claustrophobic within my own skin. I just wanted what I assumed everyone wanted—freedom to live a good life, a joyful life, a life with a sense of purpose and meaning where you know you matter to those around you.

During my week in the hospital, I realized I felt more joy and peace than I had ever felt, all thanks to the presence of God's Spirit within me. I knew Jesus had saved me and freed me from the burden of my sins and that I would one day return to that blissful place I had experienced so briefly, that panorama of beauty, color, life, and joy where God made his dwelling place. I knew he had returned me to life for a reason, presumably to tell everyone about the spiritual realities we all face after this life on earth has passed. But how and when to tell them—I wasn't sure how to begin.

For the time being, I needed to concentrate on getting stronger so I could be released from the hospital. My doctor continued to check in on me, but his visits seemed shorter each time. He continued to marvel at my recovery and say that he had no explanation for how I was able to heal so quickly. I knew the reason, of course, but again, was pretty sure he would never believe me if I told him. How could I explain God's peace that passes understanding to a man of science?

Mom and Dad came every day, and my friends from school came a few more times. They sensed something was very different about me, that I had a sense of peace and calmness that they had never encountered in me before, but they attributed it to my injury and the pain medication. Mom had attempted a couple of times to "really talk" about why I did what I did. But I didn't know where to start—with competing for attention with my brothers and sisters? With her divorce from my father? With all the years of hurt feelings and crushing disappointments?

"I'm sorry, Mom," I said both times she asked. "I'm so sorry to put you through all this. I never meant to—"

"Oh, Tam," she said, getting emotional once again. "Why would you do such a thing? What got into you? Something at school? Did something happen? Is it a boy? I saw the way they've all been flocking around you this week. What happened, honey?"

I shook my head, now able to sit up unassisted. "It's . . . it's just hard to explain, Momma," I said. "It's a lot of things."

"That reminds me—you know you're required to see a psychiatrist after you check out of here next week."

"I don't know . . . maybe," I said, shivering at the thought of trying to bare my soul to a stranger and explain my new relationship with God. If I couldn't explain it to my own mother, how was I ever going to tell someone who didn't know me at all?

Mom just shook her head and started reading through the various cards I'd received, something she did daily, though I hadn't received any more since the initial flood of flowers and well wishes came in. It was her way of stepping away from the pain of something that threatened to overtake her, as if my depression—or whatever it was—could somehow be contagious.

———

Despite my anxiety over what to tell my family and friends about what I'd experienced, my body was feeling better and better. I was eating again, finally, and by that point usually had someone slip in something from Taco Bell or Dairy Queen. I'd learned that hospital food deserved its reputation.

From the way my friends responded, I knew I, too, was developing a reputation. Some did not come back after that first visit. Others surprised me and came almost every day. But hardly any of them called me. This was in the days before social media (thank goodness!), but when the phone rang in my room, I soon learned it was probably my father, one of my siblings, or an aunt or uncle.

On the day I was released from the hospital, I had a new appreciation for time as I stared up into the faded-denim blue West Texas sky. On one hand, it felt as if only a few minutes had passed since the gun had fired into my body. On the other hand, lying on the floor of my parents' bathroom seemed a lifetime ago. So much had happened inside and yet so little seemed to have changed outside.

Rising from the mandatory wheelchair, I gripped the arm rests, still a little shaky from lying in bed for a week, and inhaled deeply.

"You okay, Tam?" Dad asked, opening the car door for me. "Take your time."

I smiled and gave him a little hug, careful to use the right side of my body.

"Yeah, Dad, I'm fine. Just glad to be goin' home."

Sunlight filtered through a lace fan of clouds and warmed my face.

I was alive.

God was with me and had given me new life.

So what was I going to do with it?

SEVEN

Body and Soul

Anyone who attempts suicide is required, by law, to meet with a psychiatrist for an evaluation. Because I was a minor at the time, this meeting was also intended to make sure I wasn't in an abusive situation at home, but primarily to assess my state of mind. If the psychiatrist deemed me at risk of hurting myself again, or a danger to others, I would be sent to the county mental hospital—a thought that reminded me of visiting hell again.

The day before I left the hospital, I was sitting up, staring at the TV, and waiting for Mom to bring me a burger, when I heard a sharp knock on my door. Before I could open my mouth to respond, a heavyset man in a dark suit pushed into my room, grabbed the metal chair from against the wall, planted it at the foot of my hospital bed, and sat down. He yanked my chart out, looked at me, and said, "Well, why'd you do it?"

How's that for an introduction?

"Umm, who are you?" I said. I already felt violated before we had even started.

He told me his name, which I don't remember, so I'll call him Dr. Jones. He wore glasses, the big oversize aviator-style frames popular in the eighties, and had a comb-over to hide the shiny dome of his balding head. He explained he was there as required by law in the state of Texas, mentioning the ordinance and statute number. He offered no identification or indication of his expertise or qualifications. Obviously, he was in a hurry, and I was not even a patient to him, just a blurred number on a chart.

"Shouldn't my mom be here?" I asked. He made me nervous to say the least. While I didn't really want Mom to listen to my attempts at answering his questions, I preferred it to being in the room alone with him.

"No," Dr. Jones said, "this is not an actual clinical session, just a preliminary intake. She can come with you next week when you visit my office." He pulled a business card from his suit jacket and tossed it into my lap. "Looks like you're scheduled to be released tomorrow. Your doctor thinks your recovery is nothing short of a miracle."

I nodded, unsure of what to say. I noticed a small coffee stain at the edge of his red tie. He just stared at me, as if we had reached a standoff in our negotiations for world peace or something equally important.

"You can tell me now or you can tell me later," he said, pushing his glasses up. "But I need to know why you tried to kill yourself or I can't sign off on your discharge, which means you will be required to spend at least a week in Pine Meadows." He seemed so pleased with himself, obviously enjoying his ability to bully an emotionally fragile teenage girl.

Fighting back tears, I turned my head away and gazed at the TV, where some contestant was jumping up and down on *The Price Is Right*. In that moment I realized my emotional recovery would be up to me and me alone. Not my family. Not my friends. And certainly not this so-called medical professional. I shuddered at the thought of walking such a painful, difficult journey alone, unable to convey all that simmered within my soul. Then I remembered that I was not alone. God was with me now. I had the healing love of Jesus filling my heart now, and I would never be alone again. Even before I discovered this verse in Scripture, I knew its truth deep inside: "Be strong and courageous. Do not be afraid or terrified because of them, for the LORD your God goes with you; he will never leave you nor forsake you" (Deut. 31:6). He understood my pain, and I knew that somehow he would see me through the difficult trials ahead.

I don't remember what else I said to the psychiatrist that day, but it was enough to make him leave. Needless to say, he was the last person I wanted to share my heart with or try to explain what I'd experienced in the afterlife. I couldn't imagine having to face him again, but his threat of sending me to our local mental hospital left me feeling like I had no options. When my mother arrived, trailing the not-so-discreet scent of onions and fries with her in a familiar white bag, I handed her Dr. Jones's card but said nothing of his visit.

———

I couldn't believe a week had passed. As we drove by the high school, I could easily imagine my friends sitting in third-period history class, whispering and passing notes, making plans for where they'd go at lunch, and who they'd take to the football game that Friday. What I couldn't imagine, however, was facing them. How would I ever go back to school and deal with the stares and whispers, the rumors and notoriety? Should I just smile and act like I'd been away on vacation or in the hospital with a bad case of flu? Just laugh it off as usual when hard things came up?

I knew there was no way to pretend things were the same, no way to deny that I was changed forever. I would just have to face them and trust the Lord to get me through it somehow. If he could save me from the eternal fires of hell, I knew he could see me through the halls of Permian High School.

At home it was as if I'd never left. Foxy barked and leaped, overjoyed to see me, as I was to see her. The big oak tree guarded our house as majestically as ever. Inside, it smelled of lemon cleaner and was just as spotless as usual, and I wondered how long it had taken my poor mother to clean the terrible mess in her bathroom. While Dad carried in the flowers and get-well gifts, I walked into my bedroom and gazed at it as if seeing it for the first time. Everything there was the same, but it seemed foreign to me, a museum of who I used to be, not the child of God I had become.

Once I was home, I soon discovered how my mom and stepdad had coped with the crisis I had triggered in our family. While I had cried out to Jesus for his mercy from the depths of hell, my parents had been pleading with him as well, begging him to save their baby girl and bring her back to them. My mother had already told me in the hospital how she assumed I would die on the way. "Your color was so pale, almost gray," she'd said. "And there was just so much blood everywhere. I was beside myself. I prayed 'cause I didn't know what else to do."

My mother had also been on her knees in their bedroom while I was recovering. She, just like her husband, had given her life to Jesus Christ, a decision she had flirted with throughout her life but now felt ready to make. They both seemed so grateful to have me home and so overjoyed that God had heard their prayers. I almost told them about my experiences while I was dead but hated to shift the topic back to me when they seemed so excited to tell me about their own relationships with Jesus.

Besides, I'd have plenty of opportunities to tell them once we were all a little more settled and back in our routine. I didn't want to freak them out and have them reconsider their decisions to welcome Jesus into their hearts. So instead, we began discussing where we should go to church. I couldn't believe the change in them already. A new life was beginning for all of us—not just for me. I couldn't wait to see what God would do next.

———

My hopeful expectations were soon tempered by the realities of returning to school and keeping my appointment with the psychiatrist. My mother had already talked to all my teachers, and they had promised to help me catch up and to give me all the time I needed to make up missed work. I knew they would be kind and sympathetic, but I worried they would pity me and treat me differently, handling me with kid gloves.

When Monday morning rolled around and Mom pulled up in front of the school, I had more butterflies than when I'd walked into a classroom for the first time as a little girl. So many thoughts and feelings competed in my mind and heart. I had started flipping through the Bible, looking for comfort and assurance, but I felt overwhelmed because I didn't know where to look. I knew God would guide me, but it would take time.

Meanwhile, I tried to hold my chin up, offer a genuine smile when possible, and act as normal as I could. I figured others would take their cues from me: if I acted okay, they would relax and return to treating me as they had before my death-defying incident. But it was exhausting.

I knew my body hadn't fully recovered from the trauma, but that first day back at school proved harder than I imagined. Most people were nice enough, but there were plenty of stares and uncomfortable silences. Maybe I was oversensitive to everyone's reactions, but it was hard to ignore the way kids averted their eyes as I walked down the hall or the way homeroom fell silent when I came through the door.

Thankfully, not everyone avoided me or acted weird. The two girls I hung out with the most tried to tease me a little but were clearly glad to have me back. And the guy who had come with them to see me in the hospital, Kyle, went out of his way to say hi and let me know he was happy to see me. Standing beside my locker after lunch, he flagged me down. "Hey, Tamara—great to see you're back. How you feeling?"

"Pretty good," I said and smiled. I was suddenly glad I had dressed up a little instead of my usual jeans and T-shirt.

"Well, you look great," Kyle said and smiled that killer smile. "What are you doin' Friday night after the game?"

"Uh, I'm not sure, probably just hanging out with Beth and Susan," I said, nervously playing with a strand of my hair. Had he ever noticed me before? Or was this just his good deed for the day, being nice to the crazy girl who tried to kill herself?

"Maybe I'll catch up with y'all then," he said. "Or maybe we can hang out sometime . . . if you want to."

"Sure, that would be great," I said, and meant it. Maybe he really did like me. I hated to blow an opportunity. The fact that this good-looking, popular football player would basically ask me out in front of everyone boosted my spirits. Little did I know the role that Kyle would eventually play in my life.

———

If the intake visit with Dr. Jones in my hospital room had been terrible, actually sitting across from him in his office was unbearable. I was just getting used to being back at school when Mom reminded me of my appointment. She told me she would pick me up after school and go with me, but my request to postpone it fell on deaf ears. "Just get it over with, Tam," Mom said. "I'll be there with you. It will be okay." I wasn't so sure. All that day, my stomach was clenched in knots tighter than the ones in my old chain necklace at the bottom of my jewelry box.

His practice was located in a brick office building near a strip mall not far from the hospital. After the receptionist checked us in, we sat in the cold, sterile waiting room that reminded me of the lobby in a cheap motel until Dr. Jones emerged from a hallway and motioned us back. He shook hands with my mother but basically ignored me. Ushering us into his office, which also reminded me of a cheap motel room, he explained that Mom could remain with me during my session, but that children were often more likely to be candid about their problems without a parent present.

Mom wasn't sure what to do and looked to me for her

cue. I nodded to let her know it was okay for her to wait, and she seemed relieved. "I'll be right out here if you need me, honey," she said before Dr. Jones closed the door behind her.

"So"—he had to look at his paperwork to remember my name—"So, Tamara, how are you doing now that you're out of the hospital and back in school?"

"Okay, I guess." I could already tell it was going to be a long fifty minutes. The room smelled stuffy, as if the window overlooking the parking lot had never been opened. Dr. Jones wore the same dark gray suit and red tie he'd had on in the hospital, probably his uniform. "You know, I'm still tired a lot, but I feel stronger and everyone at school has been nice."

"I see," he said, without looking me in the eye, content instead to scribble in his notebook. "Which brings us back to why you shot yourself in the first place."

Did it? I wasn't sure how, but it was clear Dr. Jones considered this the million-dollar question, and he was determined to get me to answer. So I talked about feeling weighted down by my emotions, the loneliness I experienced even though I had friends, the pain of my parents' divorce, all the things I suspected he wanted to hear. He nodded and mostly wrote in his notebook, rarely looking up. I felt like he was counting the minutes as much as I was.

Right before our session ended, Dr. Jones took out a little pad, scrawled his signature on it, ripped out the page and handed it to me. "You're battling severe depression. This medication will help you. I'll see you back here next week."

If I hadn't been depressed already, the prospect of coming back to endure another session with him would surely have done the trick.

On the ride home Mom quizzed me on what he'd asked and how I had responded. I sensed she was worried about how she and my stepdad would look, as if what I'd done were somehow their fault. I tried to reassure her but knew she would probably always feel guilty, the burden of a parent's love.

———

Mom didn't get the prescription filled on our way home, although she offered. I told her that I didn't want to take it—not yet at least—because I was still recovering physically. Based on what I'd heard from some of my friends who took antidepressants, I expected it would only make me lethargic and sleepy. It would be hard enough to concentrate in school when I returned the following week without feeling as if I were moving in slow motion and watching my life pass by like a parade float. I feared any medication Dr. Jones prescribed would only make my recovery harder. I also wondered if I was reacting more in fear of him than any effects the medication might have.

When we returned for my second visit, I think my mother dreaded it as much as I did. She seemed jumpy, as if Dr. Jones were about to make her defend herself as a good parent. Sitting there in the waiting room, we were both as fidgety as toddlers in a church service.

"You want to do this?" Mom asked, surprising me.

"Are you kidding? No, I hate having to do this! You saw that—that *doctor*—he creeps me out."

"You want to leave?" she whispered.

"Yes!" I said, aware of how loud my voice sounded. "Oh, thank you, Momma!"

"You don't need that psychiatrist or to be doped up on those drugs he wants to put you on. You'll be just fine— you've got Jesus!" She gathered her purse, and without saying a word to the receptionist or anyone else, we walked out, and I never returned.

Now before you start thinking that we acted rashly and that I must hate anything to do with therapy, psychiatrists, and antidepressants, let me assure you otherwise. I have the utmost respect for mental health professionals and know God has given so many of them hearts of compassion as well as heads full of knowledge. I want to make it clear that sometimes it's absolutely essential for a person to seek medical treatment to deal with depression, anxiety, and other emotional battles—even when that person knows Jesus. The body and brain can indeed develop chemical imbalances that require therapeutic remedies, without the added burden of stigma or judgment.

At that point in my young life, however, my mother and I felt completely confident that these were not what I needed. I was no longer a danger to myself or a threat to the safety of anyone else. I was a totally changed person from the girl I had been only weeks earlier. While an enormous amount of healing still needed to take place, I knew without a shadow of a doubt that this doctor and his mind-numbing meds were not the answer. I no longer wanted to escape my problems—I wanted to be whole!

I'm still a work in progress today, but even then I knew that the deepest emotional healing can only be found in God. He can use doctors, therapies, and relationships with loved ones and others to help us heal. But there is no substitute for the love, grace, and presence of Jesus in your life. Spending time with him, talking to him, listening to him, and reading the Word of God is the first course of action. It's what I needed most in my life at that point.

But I still had a way to go before I would realize this.

A long way.

EIGHT

Reentry

Returning to school remained a bittersweet experience to say the least. In many ways, my worst fears continued to play out whenever I walked into a classroom only to have it fall silent, followed by classmates staring and whispering. Behind my back a few of the jokers would even twirl their fingers beside their heads to mimic the craziness they assumed led to shooting myself. Some kids laughed nervously while others just ignored me.

Their knowing glances, awkward greetings, and polite exchanges were nothing, however, compared to the outright rejection I encountered from a few of my former friends. Some acted concerned and caring at first and then let their lack of calls and invitations reveal how they really felt. One girl flat out told me, "Look, Tam, I'm sorry for what you've been through—I really am. It's just . . . my mom doesn't want me hanging out with you anymore. She thinks . . . well, she just thinks you attract trouble."

For a select few of my peers, I became an object of sympathy or even pity. They wanted to show concern but never wanted to know what really lay beneath the surface of my desire to take my own life. Consequently, I felt I could identify more with the kids I barely knew—the "outsiders." They were not into sports and didn't belong to any other core group—stoners, extreme party types, drama queens (the Goth movement was in its infancy)—so I assumed I had more in common with them. Their defiant attitude displayed a lurking inner desire to obtain something different from life. I could relate to their attempts to escape reality, but I knew there was no way to hide from real truth. Ultimately, I knew no matter what group I associated with, none of us was really that different. The things that separated us the most were only personal interests and how we postured for the rest of our peers.

Thankfully, a handful of friends remained just that— real friends. They didn't know what to say or how to act any more than anyone else did, but they didn't let their awkwardness keep them from caring about me. For the most part, they didn't want to know about why I'd done what I'd done, or really even to talk about it. Maybe they were afraid, or simply didn't know how to ask. Like me, they wanted things to go back to normal—or, more accurately, to level off at whatever the new normal for my life would be.

When I returned to school, I had no idea how far I would

go in my desire to belong—or how long I would spend running away from the spiritual reality now at the center of my soul.

———

My transition back into the life of a teenage girl in high school wasn't made any easier by my parents' new obsession with church. Maybe *obsession* is too strong a word, but my mother and stepfather seemed bound and determined to honor the promises they each had made to God now that I had lived and recovered from my near-fatal injury. My stepfather quickly located the church I had described to him from the vision I shared when I was in the hospital, a small Bible-based church sitting on a hill in a neighboring community.

Our new church home welcomed us with open arms, and our family began attending every time the doors were open—usually three or four times a week. I was excited and curious to learn more about God after my up-close-and-personal encounter with him, but I quickly found myself feeling overwhelmed in church. Even as I was drawn to God's Word, I found church to be more of a social gathering than a pursuit of holiness. When I began reading the Bible, I had a deep connection but was perplexed about how to actually apply it to my life. Everyone at the church seemed to know so much more about the rules of "religion," and, knowing what I knew from my after-death experience, I wasn't sure the majority really understood spiritual truth.

While my mom and dad seemed to fit in at our new church home, I struggled to connect and make friends my age. There were a few other kids in the church youth group, but they seemed to have been in church their entire lives. They were quiet and polite, and I had no idea how to relate to them, or they to me. My old longing to belong and to be accepted left me feeling lonely and isolated once again. I didn't fit in at school anymore—if I ever did—and I couldn't really relate to anyone at our new church home.

It left me vulnerable. At school I began talking more with some of the wilder kids, the ones who smoked outside near the corner of the gym, who cut class to cruise and drink beer on country back roads, and who partied most every weekend. They accepted me more than anyone else, really. My suicide attempt apparently gave me credibility with them as a tough cookie; and now that I'd lived, they assumed I wanted to party as much as they did.

Boys began to ask me out. Some were "bad boys," but others were really good guys I once would have loved to date. But insecurity gnawed at my heart, and a nagging whisper in my mind reminded me of the harsh realities of rejection. *They're just trying to be nice. Once they get to know you, they'll see how weird you really are,* I told myself. *And do you really think any of them would believe you if you told them about what you experienced in hell and heaven? They would think you were crazy for sure! No, you just need to kindly turn them down. Don't set yourself up to be hurt even more.*

Of course, now I realize how the Enemy seized my

insecurities and self-doubts and used them as opportunities to undermine my new fledgling faith. The Bible tells us, "Be alert and of sober mind. Your enemy the devil prowls around like a roaring lion looking for someone to devour" (1 Peter 5:8). While he could never have my soul again, he certainly did not want me to grow in my faith or discover how to live in the power of the Holy Spirit.

So although I had died, experienced the anguish of hell, and tasted the bliss of heaven, I was still human. All the old weights of painful rejection from my family and the isolation of not belonging quickly began pressing in on me once again.

In many ways the months following my trauma sent my soul bouncing back and forth like a tennis ball. While I was part of a solid, Bible-believing church of caring people, I was secretly falling in with a group of other young adults who cared only about having a good time.

Most of my friends were beginning to experiment with drinking, which left me surrounded by the temptations of alcohol. While I was learning to pray and spending time in God's Word, I was also rebelling in my heart against the ache of loneliness that seemed all-consuming. On Saturday nights I'd go out with my friends, many of whom were drinking, even if I didn't join them; and on Sunday mornings I'd be next to my parents in the pew, worshipping and praying.

If it sounds a little spiritually schizophrenic, it was. Afraid to share the truth of all I had experienced after death, I worked at living in denial. I began playing a dual role that divided my heart between the longings of my flesh and the spiritual cries of my heart. And the tension between the two would get a lot worse. Finally I faced a crisis that would force me to choose once and for all whether I would follow God or allow my emotions to extort me into following others.

———

"That was some party after the game, wasn't it?" said Whitney. A group of friends and I were leaning against the fender of my friend Susan's Mustang at the Sonic, sipping slushies and joking about what we'd like to spike them with. We had cut last period for no good reason other than to do it.

"Hey, look who just pulled in," said Susan, pointing to a red pick-up jacked with oversize tires. "I know who he's here to see! He's got his eye on Tammy!"

I rolled my eyes and tried to ignore her teasing. Kyle and I had continued to talk and flirt ever since my ordeal. He kept saying we were going to go out, but he never got around to actually asking me out. So instead we continued to play the game teenagers play, masking our attraction to each other with nonchalance. I still hadn't gone out with any of the guys who had asked me, but I suspected that if Kyle ever got around to asking me, I'd be too weak to resist.

Sure enough, Kyle pulled in to the spot next to us, ordered a shake and fries, then got out to chat with us. He had just come from football practice and looked beat. But even sweaty in jeans and a Panthers T-shirt, he looked good. Any of my friends would've killed to date him or receive the kind of attention he'd been showering on me.

"Hey, ladies," he said, leaning on the fender beside me. Million-watt smile, straight out of Hollywood. "What's up?"

One of my friends giggled while another scooted to make room for him. He smelled clean despite being sweaty, something like citrus and spice, and I couldn't help noticing how his biceps strained the sleeves of his shirt. "You're lookin' good, Tam," he said, reaching for my slushie and popping the lid to take a sip. The raspberry flavor left him with a blue moustache, and I smiled.

"Thanks," I said. "How was practice?"

"Good," he said, returning my drink. "Coach is workin' our tails off. Gotta make State playoffs or he's gonna kill us. Same old, same old."

A server skated toward us and delivered Kyle's milkshake. He paid her and told her to keep the change, which was probably only about twenty cents, but it seemed generous at the time. His arm brushed mine and his eyes glinted like emeralds in the late afternoon sunlight.

"We better get goin'," said Susan, jangling her car keys. "Momma is gonna kill me if she finds out I skipped today."

"What's your hurry?" Kyle said.

I shrugged while my girlfriends began to pile into the Mustang.

"Tam, I'll take you home if you wanna stay and talk some more."

Susan shot me a look that said I was crazy if I didn't see how obvious he was being. "Um, okay," I said. "Sounds good—let me grab my backpack."

I don't know how much longer we lingered at the Sonic that day or when we officially had our first date. All I know is that I loved the way he made me feel. And that opened up a whole new set of problems.

———

By Christmas that year, my life resembled that of most any other girl my age. On the surface we looked like a model Christian family, always at church or prayer service or Bible study. My mom and dad seemed happy, but they also seemed a little . . . *distant.* They had accepted their new faith in Jesus like a ready-to-wear outfit straight off the rack, since they were already immersed in the culture of small-town West Texas where everyone's a Christian. The Bible, Jesus, and church were just part of the landscape, as much as oil rigs and hay barns and the sun rising over the prairie every morning. They fit in their surroundings more now than they ever had.

My new faith didn't fit as well, though. My heart was constantly divided by two forces pulling at my focus. I had started praying more regularly, asking God to help me, to teach me, to counsel me so I could be healed of all the pain that continued to plague me. But my self-incrimination, loneliness, and desire to be accepted and loved continually pulled me like gravity into the world of high school popularity.

Kyle and I had started dating sporadically. Looking back, it's easy for me to see the mixed messages he gave and how they left me confused, frustrated, and anxious. We would go out a few times, and he'd make it clear that he was really into me and would like us to date exclusively. He would sweet-talk me and say that's what he wanted, and then he wouldn't call for days.

When I would finally run in to him at school or someone's party on the weekend, he would grin sheepishly, flash those twinkling green eyes, and tell me how busy he'd been—but also how much he had been thinking about me and missed me. I'd be drawn right back into his orbit, the moth to his flame, and be waiting when he came to pick me up the next night. Gradually, our relationship became more physical as I instinctively became willing to do whatever it took to receive the love I so desperately craved from him.

Even after I heard I was not the only girl Kyle dated and played his little passive-aggressive game with, I couldn't give him up. Somehow he would smile that killer smile that seemed to melt all my defenses, and I'd feel weak and needy. I hated myself for it, but nonetheless I couldn't give him up. He made me feel special and beautiful. Because he was a popular, good-looking, well-liked football player, my confidence went up whenever I was with him.

So I kept hiding from the truth. As if I were wearing a blindfold that couldn't keep out the light in front of me,

I tried to make my life work the way I wanted it to. Even though I loved God and knew he had chosen me to return to this earth for a special purpose, I couldn't figure out how to shed my fears and insecurities. As a result, I allowed my craving for the approval of my peers to muffle God's voice that continued to echo inside my heart.

———

I resisted taking responsibility for my relationship with God and for the health of my soul. I knew he could reach inside my heart, instantly heal all the wounds there, and make me whole—which I naïvely assumed meant feeling happy all the time, or at least most of the time. Knowing the power of God to rescue me, literally, from the depths of hell, I knew he could heal me and provide everything I longed to have in my life. My family would love and accept me the way I wanted them to, my friends would all want to be around me, and Kyle would come to know the Lord and care for me the way I was beginning to care for him. Yet it didn't seem to be happening—at least not the way I imagined.

So I became confused and couldn't understand why God would not take away my pain and fix my problems—a response that seems a little embarrassing and immature to me now as I look back at this season of my life. But at the time I questioned God for not healing me and revealing himself in my life the way I wanted him to. Obviously, it was much easier to make excuses for myself and blame God for my lack of spiritual growth—it always is—than to take ownership and spend time with him in worship, prayer, and in his Word.

Blaming God along with the people around me allowed me to justify my rebellious heart that only wanted to numb the pain and escape from the truth. Basically, I got in my own way and prevented God from the restorative work he had started and wanted to continue. So I continued partying and running around with Kyle, trying to get my emotional and spiritual needs met through the approval of others instead of immersing myself in the truth of my new identity in Christ. This was the only way I knew to address my problems—the only way to cope with the old issues, as well as with the new secret I now carried.

The irony is not lost on me now, though I couldn't see it then. There I was, given a second chance at life, a second chance at heaven, and yet I was afraid of what others would think of me and how they might reject me. I couldn't bear to tell them of my supernatural experiences. While I didn't doubt the absolute truth of that spiritual reality I'd encountered on that bathroom floor, I did doubt others' willingness to believe me. So I was pulled in by a riptide of painful emotions.

Although I now had the love of Christ in my heart, and even though I knew my sins had been forgiven and that one day I would return to heaven as my everlasting home, I couldn't let go of my own attempts to fill the emotional void in my life. Down deep, somewhere in the back of my mind,

I knew that the Holy Spirit was the only one who could fill my need for love and intimacy. But instead I trusted in my own abilities and pursued filling that need through Kyle and other friends. I can relate entirely to what Paul wrote: "I do not understand what I do. For what I want to do I do not do, but what I hate I do. . . . For I do not do the good I want to do, but the evil I do not want to do—this I keep on doing" (Rom. 7:15, 19).

As the months flew by, I felt even more torn. After living my double life this way for so long, I couldn't imagine how anyone would believe me if I told them I had died, experienced hell and heaven, and had been given a second chance. Everyone at school knew I liked to hang out with rebels and partyers. They all knew about my on-again, off-again relationship with Kyle. While I wanted to care more about what God thought of me, I couldn't make myself stop caring what other people thought.

I felt trapped—even more confined than when I had shot myself.

I had tried dying, and it didn't work.

But living didn't seem to be going so well either.

I was stuck.

NINE

What Happened to Me?

More than a year had passed since that day I had locked myself in my parents' bathroom and held a .38 to my chest. So much had changed in that year's time, but I often felt that everything was the same. The biggest change was that God's Spirit now dwelled in my heart. Though I still struggled with my tendency to please others and want their approval, I knew without a doubt that my heavenly Father's love was all I truly needed. Nevertheless, I often felt frustrated, caught between the magnetic pull toward my peers and the eternal anchor I now had in Jesus Christ.

Sometimes I would stare at myself in the mirror, after showering or while getting dressed, and gently place my finger in the scar of the bullet hole. In church I had heard the story of Christ's resurrection and how he appeared to his disciples in the Upper Room where they were hiding out.

Jesus suddenly showed up in their midst even though the door was locked and their location was a secret. The Lord knew that one of his followers, Thomas, wanted proof that his master had truly risen from the dead. And as we see in Scripture, Jesus offered that proof:

> [Thomas said], "Unless I see the nail marks in his hands and put my finger where the nails were, and put my hand into his side, I will not believe."
>
> A week later his disciples were in the house again, and Thomas was with them. Though the doors were locked, Jesus came and stood among them and said, "Peace be with you!" Then he said to Thomas, "Put your finger here; see my hands. Reach out your hand and put it into my side. Stop doubting and believe."
>
> Thomas said to him, "My Lord and my God!" (John 20:25–28)

I touched my scar to remind myself of the truth of my own death and second chance at life, both here on earth and also for eternity in heaven. Even as the physical wound healed and the scar faded, I knew the change in my soul would last forever. I knew God had restored me to life for a reason, and I desperately longed to fulfill that purpose and tell others about the grace beyond belief he had given me. But the longing to fit in lingered, and so did the conflict in my soul.

———

Perhaps the best example of my conflicted heart emerged in my ongoing, hot-cold, push-pull relationship with Kyle. I was caught up in the cycle that so many of us, especially young women, fall into with destructive and emotionally abusive relationships. I thought I needed Kyle's attention, affection, and what I thought was his love—but wasn't really healthy, godly love. If I had that, I felt I was okay. Looking back, I try to have compassion for my fragile, teenage self, knowing that when you're starving for something, even an unhealthy relationship seems better than nothing.

I assumed that if he liked me, found me attractive, and wanted to be with me, I must be worthy. If not, my deepest fear was true—no one could really know me and love me. I knew in my mind and soul this wasn't so, because I knew God valued me—enough to send his Son Jesus to die for my sins and enough to rescue me from hell and bring me back to life. But in my heart I struggled to hold on to this awareness of my true worth. So when Kyle was calling, I felt happy. When he ignored me and began chasing after some other girl, I was left feeling like a failure, unworthy of anyone's love—all the old feelings that used to squeeze me so tight.

This spirit of rejection and abandonment would speak up any time I even considered telling anyone the truth of my after-death experience. Like a bully taunting me in the playground of my mind, a barrage of lies washed over me, intending to suppress the truth by using my own weaknesses against myself.

No one is ever going to believe you, so why make a fool of yourself? If you feel rejected now, just imagine being labeled a crazy, a social outcast for the rest of your life! Who would want to be associated with someone like that? Look at how you're living—you're terrible! No matter how much time passes, you will never escape what you did. Your family is still ashamed of you. Your friends will never accept the real you. Kyle already can't stand you most of the time. Face it, Tamara, you're never going to belong!*"*

Later, I would see how my emotional turmoil left me vulnerable to the Enemy. The Bible says, "Do not give the devil an opportunity [to lead you into sin by holding a grudge, or nurturing anger, or harboring resentment, or cultivating bitterness]" (Eph. 4:27 AMP). Other versions (such as the NLT and TLB) translate "opportunity" as "foothold," which provides a concrete picture of how our sin provides a landing point, a kind of stepping stone, for the Enemy in our lives. I left the door of my heart open just enough for him to wedge his lies into my life, keeping me divided and preventing the spiritual growth that would see through these snares.

Nonetheless, God did not desert me. I could still feel his presence with me whenever I stilled my mind and heart before him. Daily, my prayers reflected the cries of my soul as I continued to ask him for healing and mercy. I prayed for strength to overcome my dependency on the approval of others. I begged to be set free from the self-imposed prison that confined me, fully aware he had already set me free and loosed the chains. Even though I knew he heard me, when I didn't feel any different and the pain once again ricocheted inside like the bullet that temporarily ended my life, I remained stuck.

After all God had done for me by giving me a second chance, I feared I was throwing it away. And that only made me feel worse, which fueled more attempts to run away from myself. My emotional riptide continued to pull me under its swirling current even though I knew my Savior would never let me go.

———

"C'mon, Tammy!" my friend Craig yelled. "It'll be fun!"

"I don't know . . . I really should stay," I said. "After all, I'm not a senior—yet."

"Oh, who cares, right? You hang out so much with us, we forget you're still just a junior—besides there are other juniors coming. We're going to Sara's house—her parents are out of town right now. She wants us to help her host and make sure everyone behaves themselves!" He laughed. "Maybe sip a little peach schnapps—maybe go four-wheeling at the caliche pits!"

I smiled. Though we usually enjoyed mild weather even in December, it really didn't matter because we never let the temperature keep us from having fun outside, especially at the caliche pits. Caliche, a sedimentary rock full of calcium carbonate, formed huge deposits throughout our area. These formations were often soft, resulting in huge pits carved over time by wind and water.

One set of pits beyond the outskirts of town was a favorite hangout, so far in the boonies that we didn't have to worry about disturbing any neighbors or having the cops show up. We'd go there and have bonfires or cookouts; some kids drank and partied there, while couples often went there to wander into the secluded areas behind the rock pits. The thought of four-wheeling through the caliche pits made me happy; it would be a fun diversion from the classroom boredom that had set in by the end of that fall semester.

Permian was a huge high school, about three thousand kids, and there was always something going on. The crowd I knew best was more like a dozen, part of a network of maybe a hundred students who had enough friends and family in common to form our own little community. We weren't really wild, and most of us got along with all the other cliques—the jocks, band people, nerds, partyers, cowboys, and rich kids. We only had one more day until the holiday break, but somehow a majority of seniors decided that their vacation should start earlier, thereby sanctioning a "senior skip day," a Permian tradition.

"Okay—I'll do it!" I said. "Just let me grab my purse and call my mom and tell her not to pick me up."

"That's my girl," Craig said. "Meet me at the car—you know, where I usually park."

Craig and his buddy Tyler were two of my closest friends. They were both sweet guys from good families.

They made good grades and kept a low profile. I harbored a bit of a secret crush on Craig but felt he was out of my league, so I settled for the relaxed friendship that had developed between us. He always made time for me and wanted to know what was really going on inside me. Craig constantly encouraged me and told me how much he liked my positive attitude and constant smile. As I think about it now, I see he must've had a little crush on me, too, because he always wondered what I saw in Kyle.

Dashing through the crowded halls toward my locker, I tried not to think about the potential consequences for skipping most of my classes that day. Fumbling with my lock, I felt a hand on my shoulder and smelled a familiar spicy cologne.

"Hey, you goin' out to the caliche pits? It's senior skip day! You can ride with me if you want."

I didn't have to turn around to know who it was. Kyle was standing so close I could feel the heat of his body. I was still pretty ticked off at him for not calling the past couple of weeks.

"Yeah, I just talked to Craig," I said. "I really shouldn't—"

"Why do you hang out with that loser?" he said as I turned to face him. "Sorry—I know he's your friend. It's just . . ."

"Yeah, he is my friend," I said, happy to see Kyle's jealous streak. "He doesn't forget to call me for weeks at a time."

Kyle made a fist and punched the locker beside me so hard I winced.

He took a deep breath and said, "Look, Tam, I'm sorry,

okay? Just been busy. End of the season, final exams, all that stuff seniors gotta do."

I nodded and searched his eyes. "Busy," I said.

The halls began to clear out as second period was about to start. "You know how much you mean to me. Yeah, I get busy sometimes, but you're the only one I really want to hang out with. Why else would I keep comin' back? We both know I don't have to." He leaned in to kiss me and I turned my head, not wanting to get in trouble if a teacher saw us. Plus, his ego was unbelievable.

"You go ahead," I said. "Maybe I'll see you out at the caliche pits later, okay? I gotta get to class."

He looked genuinely hurt. "Sure. But remember what I said—I meant it." He walked away, and I waited until he turned the corner before grabbing my purse and slamming my locker closed. I began walking toward the cafeteria just as the bell rang signaling second period.

Classroom doors were all closed now. I should have been in Algebra 2 trying to make sense of polynomial equations, but instead I was trying to identify other, more personal, unknown variables. I knew better than to trust my heart, but still . . . it would be so fun to just forget all my problems for a little while. Besides, Craig was waiting on me, and I hated to leave him in the lurch. Maybe I would just ignore Kyle the same way he had ignored me, make him grovel a little more.

There was a pay phone on the wall in a little alcove before the double doors of the cafeteria. In a pre-cell-phone world, this was where students made calls. I dropped in my quarter, dialed home, and tried to steady my nerves for the unknown outcome. My mom answered on the first ring.

"Hey, Mom, it's me," I said, trying to catch my breath and sound normal.

"Is everything okay? Are you sick?" Mom said, now always on high alert in unexpected situations.

"I'm fine—just calling to tell you I'm hanging out with Craig after school, so you don't need to pick me up—and actually, it's senior skip day so I'm going to ditch. You know, everybody is." I realized then my head ached and I felt a little dizzy anticipating how she might respond. "Okay?"

"Senior skip day, huh? But you're just a junior," she said.

"I know, but most of the juniors hang out with seniors so all my friends are skipping too. No big deal," I said, trying to sound casual about it all.

Silence. My vision went blurry as I leaned against the cold, painted-cement wall of the cafeteria.

"Well, I guess it's okay," Mom said. "But don't forget you need to finish your laundry—you left a big pile of it on the floor—and get your research paper written. I want you home by supper, okay?"

"Yes, ma'am," I said, releasing a silent sigh of relief. "Thanks, Mom! Love you!"

"Bye, Tam."

I placed the phone back on its receiver and turned to go find Craig. But before I could take a step, I lost my balance and fell into the wall. Even though my body felt weak, in my mind I had a clear sense of warning about the decision I was making. I closed my eyes and glimpsed the future. If I skipped my classes and went with my friends, I knew my life would never be the same. I had a keen sense of foreboding, like the scent of ozone before a cloudburst, that something life-altering would happen if I went out to the caliche pits that day.

Opening my eyes, I had a second, equally strong understanding of what would happen if I stayed. I saw myself back in class, at a desk, watching the teacher. But such a decision would mean ditching my friends and risking their rejection. This scene carried a sense of peace and stability, an awareness that I would be giving up my friends but gaining something else. I was at a spiritual crossroads, and the stakes had never been higher.

"There you are!" Craig said. "C'mon, let's go, Tam!"

"Sorry," I said. "Had to call Mom. Didn't mean to keep you waiting."

And I followed him out the door.

———

I wouldn't recall that warning until many months later. For the rest of that day, I simply put it out of my mind and assumed it was the result of my overactive conscience about skipping, even though my mother knew about it and had agreed to it. Instead of heeding the cautionary vision of the Holy Spirit that day, however, I distracted myself by sipping a strawberry wine cooler and laughing with my friends at

Sara's house. We played Christmas music and acted silly with a couple of Santa hats someone brought. It didn't take long until there were more than fifty teenagers filling the living room. Between the noise of voices and at least two different boom boxes playing, no one could hear themselves think.

Finally, Sara stood on the dining table and yelled, "Hey y'all! Cool it! I don't want the neighbors callin' the cops on us. Let's move the party to the caliche pits!" Everyone embraced the idea. Craig and I helped Sara encourage our friends out the door by reminding them of the four-wheeling competitions that typically took place out at the pits.

We arrived just in time to watch the sun set along the horizon, a golden thread stitching the earth to the sky. Some of the guys gathered wood and piled it in the rock circle of an old fire pit. Others sat on tailgates of pickup trucks, talking and enjoying themselves. Most were drinking out of red Solo party cups or beer cans. A few of the girls smoked cigarettes while most of the guys preferred chewing tobacco, proud of the faded-out circles their Skoal cans left on the rear pockets of their Wranglers and Levis. No one was out of control, just a bunch of happy teenagers enjoying themselves.

Craig and I were handed red cups, which we filled with Coke, and we began to mingle, talking to friends. As more people began to arrive, someone tuned their car radio to a country station. We began to sing along and the girls began to dance—but not the macho guys, of course. Then the station was switched to pop, and we all started singing "Don't you forget about me!" in unison with the theme song from the movie *The Breakfast Club*, which had come out earlier that year. The song perfectly expressed the sentimental fears of the soon-to-be graduating seniors and their intent to make sure no one ever forgot them.

"I'll be right back," said Craig, and he headed off toward the hedge of the tumbleweeds. I smiled and strolled back to his car so I could sit on the trunk. It felt good to be part of the group. Sure, I felt guilty for being there, but it would be my last chance to see a lot of them before Christmas. I just prayed nothing bad would happen and that my parents wouldn't find out I was there with so many kids who were drinking. Even though I wasn't drinking much at all, my parents would fear the worst if they heard I was at a party with a bunch of seniors out at the caliche pits.

"There you are! I thought you weren't going to come."

I squinted through the dusky twilight and smiled up at the familiar face. "Changed my mind," I said. "A woman's prerogative, I think they say."

"Uh-uh," said Kyle, grabbing my hand and gently pulling me to my feet. "You remember what I said?" He leaned in to kiss me, and I let him this time.

"Yeah, I remember." I put my arms around his neck and hugged him close.

"I've missed you," he said. "You're so special to me."

"I missed you too."

"Let's go to my house," he said. "My parents went to Lubbock and won't be back until tomorrow."

"I don't think so . . . I told Mom I'd be home for supper. Plus Craig is going to help me with my English essay."

He laughed. "Even you gotta admit those are lame excuses, Tam!"

I had to laugh too.

"Okay," I said. "But just for a little while."

At the time, that day seemed magical. But its magic didn't last long.

———

After the holidays Kyle told me he needed some space, some time to think about what he wanted to do with his life after graduation. Soon he was up to his old tricks, and I had to battle the feelings of rejection and heartache that rose within me. School dragged on, and I became more and more insistent with my prayers for God to deliver me from my reliance on people.

Church was good, but there wasn't anyone there my age. A few families had really young kids, and the rest of the members were my parents' age and older, empty nesters or retirees. Being the baby in my family, I always felt I had missed the opportunity to connect with my considerably older siblings. So I longed to be around other young adults with whom I could relate and connect. Friends like Craig attended church and certainly shared Christian morals, but I didn't know anyone from school who was serious about knowing God. I'm sure they were there, but I didn't know how to find them. My parents loved our church as much as I did, and we all knew it was the place we belonged, so I didn't complain.

Meanwhile, I continued to feel confused about why God wouldn't take away my emotional dependency on Kyle and my other friends. I soon suspected the stress was affecting my health because I began to lose weight. Nothing tasted good to me anymore. Then I began gaining weight, which I knew must be bloating, because I wasn't eating much at all. In February I missed my monthly visitor and wondered if something were seriously wrong with me. After all, my nerves were certainly shot and my stomach stayed in knots— but what if it were more than just the emotional struggle?

Like everything else I didn't like, I tried not to think about it. But then a few months later in early May, I went shopping with Mom for a dress for prom. To my surprise, Kyle had asked me and claimed I was his first and only choice. I said yes, of course, and didn't care whether I was the first girl he asked or not, because I was the one who would be on his arm when he walked into the Panthers gym in his rented blue tux.

"Do they have this dress in a bigger size, Mom?" I asked, handing her several others that didn't make the cut.

"Let me check," she said, handing me a couple more to try.

But none of them fit me. I had always been able to wear my size off the rack without alterations, but now something was up.

"I've been wondering if you gained a little weight, honey," Mom said, handing me a larger size of the long red dress I liked. "But yet you don't seem to be eating much at all." I let her into the dressing room again. We didn't say anything, but both of us stared at my slightly extended stomach. We looked up at each other without saying a word.

In that moment the truth hit us both.

I was pregnant.

TEN

To Tell the Truth

On the way home when my mom asked me if I could be pregnant, I told her I had taken a test the month before, which was negative. "But you *were* takin' a test, right?" she said. "Which means you knew it's possible." She shook her head and I assumed she would be furious. Instead, I saw tears stream down her cheeks. I began to cry as well.

"I'm . . . I'm so sorry, Momma," I said. "It's not what you think . . ."

"Kyle?" she said, trying to hold back her anger toward him.

I nodded.

"I'll make you an appointment and take you to see Dr. Stevens next week. Don't say anything to your dad until after we go to the doctor."

I nodded again and wiped away my tears.

We drove in silence the rest of the way home. I stared out the window and thought about how happy we had been on the way to shop for prom dresses. And now I felt so bad. I had disappointed my mom and dad, but worse I had disobeyed God. In my way of thinking my new condition was the direct result of my weakness, my need for love that had compelled me to lower my standards. Even before shooting myself, I had always thought I would save myself for my future husband. As much as I liked boys, hanging out with Craig and Tyler, and as much as I cared for Kyle when he treated me right, I never considered reaching the point where I now found myself.

As much as I wanted to blame Kyle, I was frustrated with myself most of all for being so weak. I was there and had allowed things to go too far on senior skip day. I recalled my warning from the Holy Spirit while standing in the cafeteria that day, right after phoning my mom. I had been at a life-changing crossroad then, even if I couldn't see it at the time. Now it made complete sense. Not only would my life never be the same, but I would also be bringing another life into this world.

Once again, I had messed up, and so many lives would never be the same. My soul cried out, *Lord, where are you?*

———

The end of the school year was usually a bittersweet time for me, bringing a sense of closure while also welcoming in the fun of summer. Being friends with so many seniors that year, I was especially sad knowing many of them would move away for college or jobs or the military. And while I wasn't looking forward to spending my pregnancy in the desertlike heat of the West Texas summer, I was grateful that I wouldn't be in school.

My appointment with Dr. Stevens confirmed what I already knew in my heart as well as because of my rapidly changing body. The worst part of that visit, however, was not having the news confirmed but enduring the contempt and judgment of the heavyset, middle-aged man. He treated me like I was the town tramp instead of a young, frightened teenager who had made a mistake and was wracked with grief because of it. The tone of his voice, the look in his eyes, even the words he chose all conveyed a biased dismissal of me as a human being. His contemptuous judgment made a painful situation even harder.

His scorn wasn't reserved only for me. Clearly, the doctor judged Mom to be a poor parent, a failure as a mother, to let something like this happen. My mom's not one to take flak from anyone else, but I guess she felt too numb to put up a fight. During the past week, she and I had each gone through the motions of our usual routines, bound by a secret. Visiting the mean, judgmental doctor and hearing his spiteful words made my situation a harsh reality. My mother and I both suffered through it, though. We had no choice.

On the way home, Mom and I once again remained silent, processing the gravity of this new reality. "Let me tell your dad," she said as we pulled in the driveway. "I'll do it tonight. He'll be crushed. It may take him a little while to talk about it—the baby. But he loves you, and he'll stand by you. We'll make it through this. Have you told Kyle yet?"

"No," I said. "I . . . I wanted to be sure before saying anything. He and I, we're supposed to go pick out a prom tux for him tonight. I'll try to tell him then."

She sighed. "Do you have any idea what he's going to want to do? I know it's been on-again, off-again with y'all, but have you two talked about marriage or anything like that?"

We got out of the car and leaned against it. A cool breeze rustled my hair on that already hot May afternoon. Foxy was barking inside, happy to welcome us home.

"I don't want to marry Kyle, Momma," I said firmly. "Even if he offered, which I'm pretty sure won't happen. He's leaving for college after graduation, and the last thing he would want is a wife and baby."

Mom nodded and took this in. "Well, you're obviously going to keep it. Don't let him—or his parents—talk you into anything. This is not what we planned, but we'll just trust the Lord and welcome this new life into our family. With or without Kyle."

I started to cry and hugged her. "Thank you, Momma."

———

When I told Kyle the news, well, let's just say it wasn't what he wanted to hear. At first he thought I was joking, but then when his grin didn't ignite a smile and laughter from me, he clenched his jaw and looked into my eyes, realizing my announcement was the truth. His green eyes sparked with flecks of light from the neon lights of the strip mall where we sat parked. We had just picked out a royal blue prom tux and ruffled white dress shirt in a shop a few yards away.

"That's some graduation present, Tam. How did this . . . I mean . . . you know, what . . . what are you gonna do?"

Just like that, in a matter of seconds, our baby had become my responsibility. His response didn't surprise me, but it did disappoint me.

"I'm going to have a baby, Kyle," I said. "I'm due at the end of August."

He stared at me as if I had started speaking ancient Hebrew.

"You don't have to keep it—I'll man up and take care of whatever things cost."

I shook my head, already prepared for such an offer.

"No, I *do* have to keep it. I *want* to keep it. God has given us a new life, a baby. It's not a problem that we can erase, I don't believe in—"

He held his hands out, palms up. "Okay, okay, I get it. But what do you expect from me then? I mean, we've had some great times this year, but a baby . . . that's like a permanent thing, you know?"

I fought the impulse to laugh. "Yes, I do know. I don't expect anything from you as far as the baby is concerned. Let's go to prom just like we planned. Smile for the photographer. And then you can go to Dallas or Austin or wherever it is you decide to go."

"Your parents know?"

"Yes, they do, and while they're not thrilled, they've made it clear they'll stand by me. They're excited about having a grandchild." I was stretching it a little by saying that, but I didn't want him to think I needed him any longer for anything.

He started his car and drove me home.

Before I got out, he kissed my cheek.

"I'm sorry," he said.

"Don't be," I said. "It will be okay."

And while I wasn't sure how it would be okay, I trusted the same God who had brought me back from the dead, from the smoldering pits of hell, to sustain me through this next season in my life.

———

There's nothing like motherhood to make you grow up fast, or at least make you feel like you are. But even as I made peace with the reality of having a baby, I felt the old pangs of loneliness, fear, and isolation. While I still hung out with most of my friends once school was out, I no longer drank alcohol or remained near anyone who was smoking. I told my closest girlfriends about the baby, and they were mostly sympathetic, while a few others used it against me, of course, judging me much like the doctor had at that first visit. Regardless, though, I was now different. I couldn't drink and pretend to fit in, because I didn't. I was going through something most of my friends wouldn't experience for years to come.

In the middle of it all, I tried to seek God. I continued going to church and prayed more than ever. My parents participated in weekly prayer meetings faithfully, like one they had hosted where a man had prayed, and God miraculously healed Mom's rheumatoid arthritis. I went with them sometimes, but an invitation to hang out with Craig or to attend someone's pool party often pulled me away. Looking back, I can give myself a break for preferring to be with my peers rather than a group of people my parents' age in a prayer circle. After all, I was a teenage girl. But at the time, I almost always felt guilty, as if I was letting the Lord down and disobeying him because I was choosing to spend time with my friends instead of him.

Then one night my parents left for a prayer meeting, and I was proud of myself for deciding to stay home instead of going with them or hanging out with friends. Part of it was that I didn't feel great physically, but I also wanted to stay home and just spend some quiet time alone. For once, I hoped to just pray and talk to God, maybe read my Bible or listen to some praise music. I was really looking forward to this because for some time, I'd felt that the time had come to tell other people about my after-death experiences. I wanted to pray for strength to finally do it. Whether it was the pregnancy or just a growing awareness that the longer I waited the harder it would get, I wanted to depend on God more. I wanted everyone to know what he had done for me, the gift of life he had given back to me, along with a glimpse of the eternal glory of heaven, the place I would one day call home.

My parents left, and the night began quietly enough. I sipped some iced tea and put on a T-shirt long enough for me to sleep in. I deliberately left the TV off and just sat—or maybe *sprawled* is a better word—on the sofa and tried to still my heart before God. I thanked him for the many blessings in my life, for my parents, my friends, and for this new life inside me. I praised him for not giving up on me no matter how many mistakes I made or how far I seemed to drift from him at times.

WHAM! I heard the sounds of screeching and wood splintering, and then an enormous splash. I opened my eyes—I must have dozed off in the midst of my prayer—and wondered what in the world I'd just heard. Without thinking about it, I assumed it must be a sudden thunderstorm. They can roll in quickly across the plains where we lived and unleash painfully loud thunder and torrents of cold, hail-like rain. But then looking out the kitchen window, I realized it wasn't raining. I brushed it off as nothing and went about my quiet evening.

About an hour later my parents came home and rushed into the house. "What did you do?" Mom demanded.

"What? What are you talking about? I haven't done anything!" Surprised and confused, I followed her through our house to the sunroom and saw something unbelievable. I blinked several times to make sure I wasn't dreaming or hallucinating. No, it was real.

The tail end of a pickup truck extended from the deep end of our swimming pool.

I let out a little scream and wondered what was going on. After such a dramatic racket, it was quiet except for the sound of the remaining water in the pool lapping gently against concrete and metal. Moving in slow motion, I went to the sliding glass doors leading to the pool and backyard.

The whitewashed plank fence running along the edge of our backyard lay in splintered shambles. Deep, rutted tire tracks scarred the yard my mother worked so hard to water and cut throughout our miserably dry summers. And there, with a front tire submerged in the deep-end was a dilapidated white pickup truck topped with a camper shell, looking like a giant metal turtle had nosedived into our swimming pool. The horrible, surreal scene lingers in my memory still, like something out of the movies or a story on the six o'clock news.

My mind tried to process it. But I didn't see the driver or anyone around. In that moment we realized the driver might still be in the car, so my mom rushed to dial 9-1-1. A few minutes later, an ambulance and a police cruiser, lights flashing, rushed into our driveway. The driver, an elderly man they had identified from his soggy wallet, was indeed dead. Seeing my tears, the EMT assured me that the driver was killed on impact and not because I didn't call 9-1-1 sooner.

Although it wasn't logical, my parents still seemed to

hold me responsible. But considering the mistakes I had made in the past, I could see how they could jump to such a quick conclusion. Fortunately, the sheriff's deputy jumped in and explained the situation. They had received a call for a missing person who fit the elderly driver's description. His wife was concerned because her husband was supposed to have been home many hours before. They didn't know if the driver was drunk or high, but the deputy made an assumption based on the number of empty beer cans he observed floating out of the old truck.

As the police finished interviewing us and the medical examiner took the driver's body away, I shuddered, knowing it could easily have been me or one of my friends in that situation. I wondered and worried about the driver's soul. Was he experiencing the torment I had encountered in hell or was he delighting in the joyful presence of the living God?

Though I had not had anything to do with this elderly man crashing into our pool and dying, I felt guilty. I knew deep down that I was not doing what God had sent me back to earth to do. Staring out the window in my room that night, tears running down my face, I heard a wake-up call. I had to tell people the truth about Jesus. I couldn't let others die without knowing him.

———

The following week I was surprised to hear a familiar, husky voice.

"Hey, it's me. I heard what happened—are you okay?"

While I ran into Kyle occasionally, since prom we had maintained a polite distance. Most people who knew me assumed he was the father, but no one really talked about it. In small-town Texas, the sexist double standard remained in place. Guys were expected to do things like this while sowing their wild oats. Girls, on the other hand, were judged and condemned as promiscuous for just one mistake. He was admired while I was criticized. Needless to say, I wasn't particularly happy to hear from him.

"Yeah, I'm okay, I guess," I said. "It was just a freak accident. The driver apparently had been drinking and was looking for his house in the development behind our fence. He lost control and ended up crashing through the fence and into our pool."

"Crazy," he said. "I'm glad you're okay, but I called to see if we could talk."

"Uh, sure," I said. "What do you want to talk about?"

"Actually, I told my mom and dad . . . the news . . . and they want to talk to you. They'd like you to come over and eat supper with us."

My mind raced with possible motives for their sudden interest. "Okay . . . but what do they want to talk about?"

He thought a minute and I wondered if he was still on the line. "I'll let them explain. But it's nothing bad . . . I think you should just listen and see what you think."

Think about what? I had been doing reasonably well, and the last thing I needed was more judgment from Kyle's parents—I'll call them Mr. and Mrs. Wilson—about how I was ruining their son's life. Still, my baby would be their grandchild, and I didn't want to punish them for what had happened. "When do y'all want me to come over?"

The next evening as it turned out. Mrs. Wilson planned a cookout, grilling burgers and steaks out by their pool, and both she and Mr. Wilson acted as warm and friendly as ever. Even Kyle seemed relaxed as we discussed his future plans for going away to school that fall. But eventually, the topic settled to the reason we were there. And that's when things got a little weird, particularly after Kyle excused himself and said he'd be back to say goodbye before I left. That left me sitting out by the pool with his parents. I wasn't sure if it was the smell of chlorine, my nerves, or my condition making me nauseous.

"Here, dear, let me get you some more tea," Mrs. Wilson said. She poured it from a large glass pitcher and placed it on the glass table beside me. Stars were beginning to come out. Cicadas chirped like a summer choir.

"Tammy, we've always liked you," Mr. Wilson said, smiling. "You know that, don't you?"

"Yes, sir," I said, sipping the tea and feeling its cold fingers reach down into my swollen belly.

"While you and Kyle have had your ups and downs, his mother and I have always appreciated you. You're a nice girl from a good family. Polite, smart, pretty."

Mrs. Wilson nodded and smiled so hard it must have hurt her face. I should have known something was up by the way her husband was piling on the compliments. I continued to feel a little seasick but tried to concentrate on what he was about to say, even if I didn't want to hear it.

Mr. Wilson stepped closer and leaned against the white post supporting the awning above the patio. "You and Kyle have your whole lives in front of you. He's about to go to college, and my wife and I got to talking, and we think you should have that same opportunity."

"I would like to but—"

"No, please, let me finish," he interrupted. "Tammy, we appreciate your reverence for life and your desire to have this baby. But a child is an enormous responsibility—and very costly. It can't be easy no matter how much support your parents give you. And they may not always be able to help like they want to."

I tried to struggle to my feet only to feel the baby kick instead. I wanted to stand so that I could make my exit as soon as he offered what I now expected based on his preamble.

"Mrs. Wilson and I would like to pay your way through college," he said. "We're also willing to pay you a stipend to help with your living expenses. There are so many fine schools in our great state, and I'm sure there's one that would suit your fancy. We would get you the best doctors in Dallas or Houston and make sure that you had no permanent health consequences from the procedure. You're so young—there will be plenty of time down the road to settle down and start a family. This isn't the way you want to do it. Will you let us help you?" He sounded like a used car salesman in one of the TV commercials run by the local dealerships, so slick and polished.

I didn't know whether to feel angry or just really sad. Either way, I felt tears welling up in my eyes. I started to stand again, and Mrs. Wilson rushed to help me, but I wouldn't let her.

"Mr. and Mrs. Wilson," I said, working to hold it together. "Thank you for having me over this evening. I'm sure you mean well, but I cannot accept your offer. Even though my pregnancy was unplanned, I know that the Lord knew all along about this little life I'm carrying. This baby is part of his plan—whatever that may be." I was starting to tremble and really needed to go to the bathroom. "I'm leaving now. Good night."

"Before you go, you need to know, if you don't take us up on this offer, neither Kyle nor any of us will have anything to do with you or this baby," Mr. Wilson threatened. His anger boiled over and melted away the smooth-talking veneer he'd maintained most of the night.

Without saying another word, I walked away. I got in my car and began backing out of their driveway, and that's when I felt the tears let loose. I rolled down the window and let the fresh air rush in as I smelled fresh cut grass from the manicured lawns nearby. The baby kicked again.

"God has not abandoned me," I said, resting my hand on my stomach. "And I will not abandon you."

ELEVEN

The Truth Sets Me Free

"Hi, Tamara—may I come in?"

"Mrs. Williams, hi!" I said. "Yes, of course, please come in."

"Please, call me Darlene," she said, as I ushered her into the living room.

I knew Mrs. Williams—Darlene—from my mom's real-estate office. A woman around my parents' age, she had always been warm and welcoming to our family. She was a petite lady with short salt-and-pepper hair, radiant tan skin, and brown eyes that seemed to look right into my heart, and she had been especially kind to me that summer. So I wasn't entirely surprised when she had asked, the last time I'd been in the office, if she could stop by to visit me during the next week. I thanked her, of course, and invited her to come any time.

With July rolling into August, I felt huge, and the oppressive desert heat became unbearable. That meant I spent a lot of time at home, on the couch, reading and watching TV, and basking in the cool comfort of the AC. Mom and Dad took great care of me, making my favorite meals (or whatever I was craving that day), doing my laundry, making sure I was comfortable. Nonetheless, I gladly welcomed the prospect of any visitor to break up the monotony of waiting on the baby to arrive.

"Would you like some iced tea?" I said and motioned for her to have a seat.

"Yes, that would be great—but let me get it, dear."

And before I could protest, she was in the kitchen pouring two tall tumblers of sun tea over ice. When she handed me one of the glasses, I felt like I was visiting her rather than the other way around. We made small talk for a few minutes, answering polite questions about each other's families and how the summer was going. Finally, Darlene leaned in and I sensed I was about to learn her motive for visiting.

"Tamara, I felt led by God's Spirit to come see you today," she said and smiled. "During my daily prayer time, your face has repeatedly come to mind. Even before I knew about your pregnancy, I've known God has special things in store for you. He spared your life for a reason. I believe he sent me to remind you of that."

My eyes misted with tears. "Thank you, ma'am," I said. "That's so encouraging."

"I'm not done," she said still smiling. "I came here to

pray for you and for your baby, if you will permit me to do so."

"Yes, please," I said.

Darlene pulled her chair closer and clasped my hands. Her palms were cool.

"Heavenly Father and gracious God," she began. "You alone know the plans you have for this lovely young woman and the new life she now carries. Your Word tells us that you want to give her a hope and a future, that you will prosper her and protect her. I don't know what she has been going through—but you do. Your Spirit lives within Tamara, and she wants to experience the fullness of your presence as you guide her and reveal what your future is for her. Lead her in your ways and reveal the platforms you have established for her to share the truth of your Word and the message you have given her that is hers alone to share."

Tears streamed down my face. I was squeezing this poor woman's hands so much they probably hurt by that point. I was so overwhelmed by her kindness and by the presence of the Lord there with us.

"Protect her from the Enemy, Lord, and guard her with your angels. Let her rest in your strength, and bathe her in your peace. Give her stamina for the delivery of this baby you have given her, and may this child be healthy and know your love as he enters this world. Bless her and this baby, God, and hold them close in your arms. Provide for all their needs. Show her the way and walk with her as she seeks to do your will and obey your Word. Give her the strength through the gift of tongues. Seal our time today with your joy. We pray this in the name of your precious Son, our Savior, Jesus Christ. Amen."

"Amen," I echoed.

———

The visit from Mrs. Williams lifted my spirits like no other gift a human being could give me. And I guess the reason it was so powerful is that I knew it wasn't just from her, but a message from God. He wanted to remind me that he had indeed saved me for a reason, and that it was past time to tell everyone around me the truth of my after-death experience. The Lord answered her prayer, and I was filled with the gift of speaking in tongues, a heavenly language that is discussed in the Scriptures.

During the next few months, I almost told my parents about my experiences several times, but in each case I felt enormous resistance from demonic forces. It got to be so conspicuous that I knew it wasn't just coincidence. The Devil didn't want me revealing the powerful truth of my encounter with the living God.

I know that may sound dramatic, but that is indeed what demons are—fallen angels. After my supernatural visits to hell and to heaven, I returned to life with a keen sensitivity to the spiritual world. The Bible refers to this awareness as the gift of discernment, the ability to differentiate good from evil. Even when I didn't act on this knowledge and tried to suppress it, I was usually aware of God's presence—or his absence—in the environment around me.

Sometimes I merely felt a cold chill and an awareness of evil surrounding me, and other times, the battle seemed more overt. I recall one night in particular. That day I had read my Bible, prayed, and decided that I was going to tell Mom and Dad about my experiences in the spiritual realms. Before I could, however, I found myself lying in bed in my room, pinned down, literally, as invisible forces tried to keep me from rising.

As I struggled to sit up, I suddenly saw what I knew to be demons swirling around me, leering and trying to frighten me. They had no physical bodies but emanated an intense evil intended to intimidate me. I immediately cried out to God only to have one of the demons choke me, constricting my throat so I could not speak. Needless to say, I was terrified! I had already been feeling displaced and then to be choked and held, unable to move or speak—I knew this was real and quite serious.

Unable to shout with my voice, I cried out in my heart, "Jesus, help me! Protect me, Lord Jesus!" Instantly I sensed someone enter my room, a presence that I knew was an angel from God in answer to my desperate prayer. The angel sat beside me on the bed, took my hand, and lowered his head as if bowing in prayer. In the blink of an eye, every evil spirit vanished like smoke pulled through a chimney.

I was in tears and began praying out loud, thanking God for sending this angel and protecting me from harm.

Even during all my months of disobedience, when I kept returning to my people-pleasing ways, despite my desire to please only the Lord, God never abandoned me. I promised him then that I would tell everyone—not just my parents and family—the truth of all I had experienced while out of my body that fall day almost two years earlier.

Once again, I repented of my past mistakes and my deep-seated reliance on the approval of others. I knew I had God's Spirit within me, and that all the powers of hell could not harm me. From then on, I instinctively knew that anytime the demons swarmed near, I only had to call out, "In the name of Jesus and by the power of his blood on the cross, I command you to go!"

This part of my spiritual education proved important, because the Enemy is real and wants to do everything in his power to destroy us. If you don't have faith and trust in the name of Jesus, the Devil will devour you. When God's Spirit dwells in you, however, you have authority over all principalities and powers. Nothing can compare to the resurrection power of the risen Christ. I experienced first hand that faith is the activating force of life.

After Mrs. Williams's visit, I felt even stronger and more confident, knowing that God was with me and more powerful than anything the Enemy could throw at me. I also decided that I should wait a little longer. I didn't want them to dismiss my message as simply the result of hormones or exhaustion. I wanted to be taken seriously and for my revelation to be respected.

So I continued to pray, waiting on the Lord's perfect time to speak the truth of my visit to heaven. During my times of prayer, I would often pray the Psalms, and one in particular was my favorite:

> LORD, you alone are my portion and my cup;
>> you make my lot secure.
> The boundary lines have fallen for me in pleasant
>> places;
>> surely I have a delightful inheritance.
> I will praise the LORD, who counsels me;
>> even at night my heart instructs me.
> I keep my eyes always on the LORD.
> With him at my right hand, I will not be shaken.
>
> Therefore my heart is glad and my tongue rejoices;
>> my body also will rest secure,
>> because you will not abandon me to the realm of
>> the dead,
>> nor will you let your faithful one see decay.
> You make known to me the path of life;
>> you will fill me with joy in your presence,
>> with eternal pleasures at your right hand.
>>>> (Ps. 16:5–11)

———

The arrival of my son produced a level of emotional intensity second only to my experiences in both hell and heaven.

Just as my after-death experience took me to new levels of excruciating pain before God lifted me to incomparable heights of heavenly glory, the process of labor and delivery duplicated that journey on a much smaller physical scale. After hours of hellish labor, the joy of holding that tiny infant in my arms was absolutely heavenly.

Soon we were back home at my parents' house, and I marveled at this stunning new gift God had given me. He seemed so perfect in every way. Mom and Dad were just as captivated with him as I was, and when my siblings came to visit, I wondered if I'd ever get to hold my son again. Everyone said motherhood looked good on me, that I seemed calmer and more mature. I wasn't sure whether that was true, but I did know motherhood helped me understand the parental love God has for us, his children, at a deeper level.

The days flew by, and I began to discover my new normal. I had already completed my GED over the summer, allowing me to say goodbye to Permian High School; so that fall I enrolled in the local community college. Mom had agreed to watch Chris, her new grandson, while I was in class, for which I was most grateful. So many changes seemed to happen so fast that the Lord was truly my only constant.

Walking across the campus of my community college, I realized I still could not escape being noticed. The campus was much bigger than Permian, and I was hoping to make some new friends who didn't know all about my past. But this was not the case. Even if they didn't know me, they had heard about me. Once again, I experienced a similar reception to the one I encountered right after I had shot myself and returned to high school. Some kids fell silent and shot glances, others whispered and gossiped, and some who I thought were friends ignored me.

Going back to school and dealing with old feelings of rejection caused me to remember my promise to God to tell others what happened to me two years earlier. While I often fantasized about standing on stage at a school assembly and telling thousands of classmates at once, I knew this was not the way to do it. I needed to start at home, tell Mom and Dad, and just allow opportunities to develop naturally.

One cool, crisp day that fall, I came home from school and told Mom that I wanted to talk to her and Dad that night after supper. She looked at me curiously, sensing that I had something important to say, but agreed. Until then, she told me how my son had smiled at her that day and how much she loved being able to take care of him. Holding him after his long afternoon nap and feeding him, I wondered how I would tell him someday about the journey his mother had taken before he was born.

But first things first. There was no easy way to begin this conversation, so after I had helped Mom clear the table and load the dishwasher, while Dad held his grandson who had once again fallen asleep, we sat in the living room and I began.

"I know how hard it is for you to talk about what

happened when I shot myself," I said. "But I need to talk about it with you. I need you to understand what all happened that day."

Mom looked at Dad, who stared down at the baby. I sensed their discomfort, but at long last I would not be denied this opportunity. Mom finally nodded and said, "Okay, honey, then tell us what you need to say. If you want to try counseling again . . . or whatever you need, just tell us."

"No, it's nothing like that," I said, smiling at the thought of Mom and me sitting in Dr. Jones's office that afternoon before skipping out like truant kids leaving school. "It has to do with what happened before you found me, before I called you."

The baby stirred and Dad passed him to Mom. Dad leaned forward and looked into my eyes. His eyes were misty, and I hated how painful this might be for him to recall that terrible day.

"After the gun went off, I actually . . . died. My spirit left my body."

"I don't doubt that, honey," said Mom. "When I found you—I thought, well, you looked like you were dead at first, pale and gray, and your pulse barely there."

"I don't know how long I was out of my body, but it was long enough for my spirit to end up—there's no easy way to say this. When I died, I went to hell. It was like scalding acid saturated me and burned me to the core. I was surrounded by other souls on the shore of this dark, burning, colossal lake."

Mom's eyes widened, and Dad's eyebrows shot up. I spent

the next few minutes describing my experience in hell before sharing how God had lifted me out and taken me through heaven before returning me to life in my mortal body.

"The whole thing was just . . . indescribable," I said. "I've tried to tell you how it felt, but it's almost impossible. But hell is real. And so is heaven. I know you both know the Lord but I believe God sent me back to confirm the truth about eternity. He wants me to tell other people, to warn them about the reality of eternal torment in hell or eternal joy in heaven."

I was suddenly exhausted, spent, drained the same way I had felt right after delivering my son. No one said anything. Mom kept nodding as if mentally processing all I had shared. Dad's eyes continued to search mine to see if I were really serious about all this. Finally, the baby roused and began to cry.

"I'll go change him," Mom said. "Then you can feed him." She took the baby into the bedroom, clearly grateful for the excuse to leave my story behind.

"Thank you for sharing this," Dad said. "I believe you, but I wonder why you've waited so long."

I tried to explain—about needing others' approval, about not wanting to be labeled any more than I already was, about my fears that others wouldn't take me seriously. Dad listened and continued to take it all in.

Mom returned and handed me the baby to nurse. "Thank you for finally telling us, honey," she said. "That's amazing . . . I just praise God you're alive."

I smiled and nodded. It was clear they believed me, or wanted to, but it was also evident that they didn't know what to do with the information I had just shared. The rest of the evening unfolded as usual, and it wasn't until later that night when I was lying in bed that I realized how disappointed I felt. I don't know what I had expected, but I guess something more. Here at long last I finally broke my silence and mustered the courage to try to explain my indescribable supernatural encounter, and it fell flat. Anticlimactic.

Just another story from Tamara.

Only I knew it was so much more.

———

After telling my parents and feeling disappointed by their response, I decided to tell someone I thought might better understand: our pastor. Reverend Whitaker, or Pastor Bob as he liked us to call him, was older, with a fringe of mostly silver hair around the dome of his head that reminded me of a halo. He knew God's Word, and I sensed he walked closely with the Lord and would not be shocked by what I had to share. So a couple of weeks after telling my parents, I made an appointment with Pastor Bob one afternoon on my way home from school.

"It's so nice to see you, Tammy," he said, welcoming me into his office. "How's that baby boy of yours? Please, have a seat."

"He's doing fine," I said, beaming. "Growing like a little

weed." I marveled at the hundreds of books lining Pastor Bob's shelves and wondered if he had read them all.

"So what's on your mind? How can I help you?"

I sat in the padded chair across from his desk and launched into a description of all that had led to that moment when the gun went off and all that had happened right after it. It was a little easier than the first time I had done it, but I still wondered what he would think of such an astonishing story.

But I needn't have worried. Pastor Bob listened intently, his eyes never leaving mine. He nodded and seemed to understand everything I shared. As soon as I stopped, he asked if he could pray, which made me feel very relieved. I don't remember exactly what he prayed, but I know he asked God to bless my faith and to continue empowering me with his Spirit. As we both said amen, my heart flooded with peace.

"Tammy, that is quite the amazing journey you experienced," he said. "The Lord obviously has shown you unparalleled favor."

I nodded, eager to hear his wise counsel.

"First, thank you for sharing it with me today. I know that can't be easy. Have you told anyone else?"

"Just Mom and Dad," I said.

"And how did that go? What did they think?" Pastor Bob clasped his fingers together, his wrists resting on his desk.

"They . . . believed me, I think. They just weren't sure why I was telling them or what they were supposed to do with my story. I guess I expected more, but I realize it sounds pretty fantastic—which is why, as I explained, I've waited so long. That, plus, I wasn't exactly obedient to God the way I wanted to be. And honestly, I've felt under attack by the Enemy more than once."

He nodded and leaned toward me. "None of this surprises me. Some people won't know what to do with this marvelous experience God has told you to share. But others will—others will be moved by the truth of your encounter. While physically dead, your spirit suffered before coming fully alive in the presence of God. The Lord gave you this remarkable gift, and you have to trust that his timing is perfect. You've waited until now, and he will use your story now to bless others and to draw them to him."

A huge weight lifted from my soul. I felt as if Pastor Bob understood almost everything, even things I didn't know how to express in words. He opened his Bible and shared several passages of Scripture with me that directly referred to the descriptions I had recounted about heaven and hell. Reading details and references to these two places I had visited brought even more relief. He then told me to write everything down in a journal, so as time passed my story wouldn't fade in my memory or be tainted by the influence of others.

As we concluded our time together, Pastor Bob prayed for me once again. And then, right before I stood to leave, he said, "Tammy, God has called you to share your experience with others, but don't try to tell everyone at once. Take it slow, and trust the Spirit to guide you about when and with whom to share it. Again, I commend your courage. You are such a brave young woman with an incredible faith. But focus on your relationship with God more than on how many people you tell about your past. Let them see the Lord reflected in the way you live your life. That's what will draw them to Jesus. It doesn't depend on you or how well or how often you tell your story. Just love him, and he'll show you how best to serve him."

To this day, I carry those words with me.

It's why I'm sharing all this with you now.

TWELVE

Healing

After I began sharing my story with others, the floodgates opened, and I experienced more peace than ever before. I took Pastor Bob's advice and tried not to tell everyone I met, which wasn't always easy. Sometimes I imagined directing the class discussion in my world history class to spiritual topics so I could tell about the truly history-changing realities of Jesus' birth, death, and resurrection.

Other times I thought about talking to the checkout lady at the grocery store or the young waiter at the Panther Diner. It may sound funny, but I truly felt burdened for each person I encountered, wanting them to know the truth of heaven and hell, and more important, the saving grace of Jesus Christ. But I knew if I just randomly and repeatedly shared my after-death experience with anyone and everyone, I would lessen its impact and dilute the power of my testimony.

So, as with almost every big decision, I began to pray and seek the Holy Spirit's guidance about when and with whom to share. Occasionally his guidance would surprise me, and I would indeed begin talking to someone sitting beside me at a ballgame or while waiting in line to buy movie tickets. Usually, though, it was in bigger settings—often church related or initiated by some local ministry—where I found the opportunity to share openly and honestly.

I'll never forget one of the first big audiences I spoke to: a youth group at a local church. The youth pastor there had heard about my experience through someone at our church, and I agreed to come and speak to them on a Sunday night. I still got scared, of course, as nervous about public speaking in front of a group of my peers as I was about the message I was there to share. I tried to write out what I wanted to say but got frustrated at my inability to find words to describe my experiences, especially my encounter with the living God.

As a result, I was forced to wing it, as they say—only I know that it was the wings of angels that protected and sustained me even as the Holy Spirit guided my tongue and told me what to say. That night was also the first time I became really emotional as I described holding the gun in my hand, feeling the bullet pierce my chest, and soon after suffering the scalding acid rain of hell and my awareness of being separated from God forever. Not surprisingly, even more tears ran down my cheeks as I related what it was like to be rescued out of such torment and ushered through heaven before coming back to life in my shattered body.

I don't know how many teens, along with a few parents and other adults, were there that night, but I'm guessing almost a hundred. When I began I could sense a spirit of skepticism and cynicism rising from their stares at me, but that only made me pray harder even as the words came out of my mouth. Soon you could hear the proverbial pin drop in that room, and every person in there was right beside me as I recounted my journey. And by the end of my talk, there was more crying than I had ever seen at any church service, including funerals.

More than a dozen people accepted Jesus Christ as their Lord and Savior that night and invited God's Spirit to dwell in their hearts. Several dozen more rededicated their lives to knowing, loving, and serving the Lord. Most of them thanked me as we prepared to leave that night, forever transformed by the God who had brought me there to tell them about his amazing power and love. For the first time, I knew I had done exactly what I was supposed to do, sensing the deep contentment that comes from knowing you've fulfilled the purpose for which God created you.

———

Reactions from the groups and individuals I began speaking to that year weren't always so good. Sometimes the reception was similar to what I had experienced at school after returning from my resurrection. Some people clearly did not want to hear what I had to say, while others actually laughed at me or mocked me. Some assumed I was crazy or delusional. Others listened but didn't know what to do with what I shared. And yet almost always some used my story as a lifeline to God, a catalyst for making a U-turn in their lives and running into their Father's arms.

Between being a new mother and sharing my after-death experiences, I didn't have as much time for hanging out with friends or beating myself up for wanting to do so. Instead I enjoyed a huge spiritual growth spurt, praying more than ever, sensing God's Spirit inside me, counseling and comforting me, directing my decisions and guiding my actions each day. Perhaps the change that made the most difference, however, was the amount of time I spent each day in the Bible.

Rather than simply looking for a verse or passage to reassure me or make me feel better, I began to be a student of God's Word, recognizing the way my experience of him reflected what I saw in Scripture. As I grew in my understanding and application of the Word of God, I experienced a new freedom from my fears. Although I had known for some time that fear is the absence of faith, I was finally learning how to apply faith on a daily basis rather than allowing my default-setting fears to consume me.

I can't stress enough how this important change affected me and helped me understand how important immersing yourself in Scripture and applying your faith is for everyone's growth and spiritual maturation. It's simple, really. Whatever beliefs or fears you embrace will become evident in your life; this is a spiritual principle. If you believe your fears will come to pass, they will preoccupy you and often come true because that is where you are placing your focus. Your belief system determines not only your path in life, but also your *quality* of life.

Please understand that beliefs are also different from knowledge. I fear that the belief system of so many people has become distorted. With more religions and denominations than we can even count, it's obvious that some are manipulating Scripture to suit their purposes and priorities. I realize this is a generalization, but consider this: if all the denominations that profess Christianity really believed that Scripture is all about unconditional love, we wouldn't have so many disagreements and divisions among Christians. Obviously, that's not what we see most of the time.

A bigger problem may be that so many people don't even know what they believe or how their deep-seated beliefs guide their thinking, influence their feelings, and shape their actions. The fear of rejection that ran rampant in my life for so long continues to hold millions of people hostage. We do whatever it takes to have others accept us and like us, justifying our actions and ignoring the long-term spiritual consequences.

But if we want to know God—to really know him and love him and serve him—then we must stop excusing ourselves and succumbing to relational idolatry. The only fear worth having is the reverent, awe-inspiring fear of God, the natural response to experiencing him and his presence.

Our humility before him keeps us reliant on him and the power of his Holy Spirit rather than our own abilities and resources.

When we live by his Spirit, we automatically have authority over all that stands between us and growing closer to him. Back in the garden of Eden, God gave Adam and Eve dominion over everything in the beautiful, newly created world. When they disobeyed God by eating the forbidden fruit after listening to Satan's lies, they lost their ownership of this spiritual authority. The Serpent seduced them by appealing to their emotions, telling them they were equals with God, and that they would be like God if they ate the fruit from the Tree of Knowledge of Good and Evil (Gen. 3:1–7).

The Enemy of our souls does the very same thing still. He tries to keep us bound by our emotions, so we won't walk in the spiritual authority God restored to us through Christ's death and resurrection and the gift of the Spirit. So many times I allowed myself to be consumed by the rushing current of my emotions even when they swept me away from the will of God. But I know God did not give us emotions so we could be slaves to them—our Creator imbued us with feelings to bind us together in love. In God's Word he tells us, "Beloved, I wish above all things that thou mayest prosper and be in health, even as thy soul prospereth" (3 John verse 2 KJV).

Once you take back control and exercise spiritual authority through God's Spirit, you are equipped to overcome the Enemy and claim the victory Christ won for you on the cross. God loved us all so much that he gave up his precious Son so we could be restored to a relationship with him, forgiven once and for all of the debt of sin that no one could ever pay. He sent his Spirit so we would have a comforter, a counselor, a friend, a power source, and a spiritual compass.

After I finally began fulfilling the purpose God gave me, I learned that I have to do my part in order for him to follow through on all he's promised. To prosper as God intended, I had to stand up in faith by believing and claiming the promises of God that were being fulfilled. I had to learn to be deliberate about the words I spoke—to myself, to my family, to my son, to my classmates, to everyone. I had to declare victory about every situation and trial I faced, rather than continuing to accept defeat without a fight.

Forgive me if it seems like I'm preaching, but the process of spiritual growth, which the Bible calls *sanctification*, is vital, and I'm deeply compelled to emphasize it to you. Believe me: God doesn't want to just come into your life so you can live a mediocre, play-it-safe, settle-for-less life. He designed you to embark on a glorious adventure with him and to live out the purpose only you can fulfill. He made you unique and special in ways that no other human being is made. God has already validated, affirmed, and accepted you more than any person possibly can.

It's no accident you're reading this book right now. God has his hand on your life and wants you to take him seriously. He wants you to live for him and experience true joy and satisfaction rather than chasing after what you think you want that will never fulfill you. He wants to give you life—the full, abundant life Jesus told us he came to bring.

Are you enjoying this abundant life?

Or are you settling for less than God's best?

It's not too late, my friend.

But you do have to choose.

———

In so many ways, that year was measured in growth spurts, both for me and my baby. Though I still struggled with my emotions and with various circumstantial trials, I knew I had grown spiritually even as I watched my son grow and learn to walk. Just as he transitioned from milk to solid food, my soul developed a hunger for the meat of God's Word and not merely the milk of surface skimming. I'm reminded of what Paul wrote to the early church at Corinth: "I gave you milk, not solid food, for you were not yet ready for it" (1 Cor. 3:2). After telling others about all that I had experienced after my life ended, I was ready to be nourished by the full power of God's Spirit.

In my old way of living, I was a prisoner to my addiction to the approval of others. I was more focused on fitting in and feeling good than on following God and becoming more like Jesus. I wanted all my emotional needs met without having to work on myself. I blamed others without taking responsibility to rely on God and exercise the spiritual authority he gave me.

But the more I studied God's Word, the more I met and prayed with other believers, the more I shared my amazing testimony, I experienced more spiritual freedom than ever before. I wasn't miraculously healed of all emotional wounds and delivered into some perfect state of peaceful bliss 24-7. But I was changed. I was no longer the young, desperate girl looking for love in all the wrong places. I had found the ultimate source of true love, the living water of salvation.

The process continued after I moved out of state to continue my education in Arizona. Mom and Dad decided they wanted to move with me and the baby, all of us eager for a fresh start. We not only felt God leading us there, but we also wanted to get away from a place with such a small-town mind-set. It wasn't long before we found a home church in our new town, and I began sharing my story. Soon I was asked to visit other local churches and speak to groups about my after-death trip to heaven and hell. For the first time I began seeing myself as an adult woman, not as little Tammy who was so needy and wounded.

God was doing a mighty work inside me, and I loved sharing it whenever I was given the chance. Some of my energy came from simply being a young adult, a single mom, working as a waitress or medical secretary to pay the bills, and feeling good about owning responsibility for my life. But most of it was supernatural. As I turned to God for the source of my identity, instead of by pleasing others, I discovered more of who I was created to be.

Gratitude played a big part in that discovery

process—and still does to this day. I have learned to come unto the Lord offering him thanks and praise for all things— even the hard ones, and even though sometimes I don't *feel* thankful. I have had to learn to humbly praise him simply for who he is and to rest in him and the unbelievable joy of his holy presence. Instead of focusing on my problems, worrying about what I don't have, or wondering why everyone can't like me, I focus on worshipping my Lord and honoring my King. The result, which began when I was a young woman barely in my twenties, continues to bring more lasting joy and abiding peace than I can describe.

I'm simply overwhelmed when I think about how fortunate I am to be alive today. Obviously, it was certainly not by my choice—but it was by God's divine design for my life. How could God show one person so much mercy and love when it was so undeserved? I had committed almost every sin there was to commit and a few more afterward! But when I called out to him from the depths of my despair, he heard me and rescued me from what I deserved and gave me a gift beyond anything I could imagine.

He didn't just give me my life back.

He gave me a second chance at heaven.

———

My second chance at life also allowed me to experience God's grace no matter how often I failed. God gives second, third, fourth, hundredth, and a millionth chances.

From a prodigal son to a woman caught in adultery, from one lost sheep to the thief beside him on the cross, God is relentless in pursuing his children. If you're reading the words on this page, it's not too late. No matter what you've been through—events, betrayals, heartaches, and traumas far worse than what I experienced—he can restore you. You can't imagine it or understand it, and fortunately you don't have to. You simply have to let God do it.

While it rarely happens instantly, you can still take comfort in knowing that he's already at work in your life. You can spend time with him and get to know him better, praying and praising him for all he's done. And you can learn more about how the spiritual realm operates within you and around you by reading the truth of God's Word.

In fact, the single greatest resource for my emotional healing was the Word of God. Obviously, God's Spirit is the primary source of healing, but the Bible has power that complements all he wants to do in you. I had to learn how to receive God's Word in my life in order to live by faith. In the Bible he tells us, "Faith is confidence in what we hope for and assurance about what we do not see" (Heb. 11:1).

Living by faith requires suffering at times. It requires discipline. It requires not allowing emotions to dictate actions. In other words, I'm not going to get all my needs met the way I think they should be met when I want them to be met. I have to trust that God is meeting and will meet all my needs—no matter what I feel like in that moment. I learned that, like the clouds of a storm front moving across the mountains of my heart, moods change, one minute sunny and circumstantially happy and the next stormy and depressed.

On the other hand, God never changes. He is the same yesterday, today, and tomorrow (Heb. 13:8). And the power of his Word never changes. It is sharp and piercing and able to divide and conquer all things if we allow the Spirit to wield it within us (Heb. 4:12). Because when we live by God's Word inside our hearts, our actions will also conform to God's ways. His Word has the healing power to set us free from our pain and sorrow.

It may sound simplistic, but without a doubt the Word of God has enabled me to become more than a conqueror through the victory of Jesus Christ and the power of his Spirit (Rom. 8:37). By reading Scripture, meditating on it, applying it to my life, and living according to its wisdom and instruction, I have attained healing I never could have imagined back when I was that teenage girl locking herself in her parents' bathroom.

Even then, God was, and has always been, at work in my life. His mercy is continually pouring out over me on a daily basis.

I had to change the way I thought about my feelings, which in turn often changed how I felt, which led to making better, more God-honoring decisions about my actions. I had to shift from dwelling on the past—either old wounds from childhood or recent slights from others—to being alive in the present. The summer breeze cooling my bare arms in the desert heat. The sound of my son's laughter as I watch him toddle across the floor into my waiting arms. The taste of lasagna I made by following my mother's recipe the first time. The joy of making a new friend.

You have the same opportunity for healing in your life. The God I served then is the same one I serve now, and he's waiting on you to come home to him and be set free from the bondage of sin and slavery in your life once and for all. You were not born into this world to suffer through a miserable, unhappy existence. God wants you to rejoice daily in the abundance of his blessings. To be alive in the present moment, *right now*. To use your senses to soak in the divine details of God's masterpiece in progress all around you.

I challenge you to stop what you're doing right now. Put down this book or close your phone or tablet. Close your eyes. Take a deep breath—really deep. Clear your mind of all the demands, worries, and responsibilities overflowing your weary soul. Rest before God and silently tell him where you are and what you need. Confess those areas where you've relied on your own selfish efforts, where you've succumbed to sin instead of standing strong in your faith. Open your heart wider than it's ever been opened. Ask for a fresh anointing of God's Spirit. Can you feel his love washing over you?

Healing is possible for you, for me, for all of us. We serve an amazing God who wants us to live our lives to the fullest. He can redeem the most painful traumas of your life and resurrect the hope that you've allowed to die. He can heal you physically, emotionally, psychologically, and spiritually. You can go from death into new life, leaving the past behind and soaring into the hope of a heavenly future. Like the psalmist, you can sing out:

> Praise the LORD, my soul;
>> all my inmost being, praise his holy name.
> Praise the LORD, my soul,
>> and forget not all his benefits—
> who forgives all your sins
>> and heals all your diseases,
> who redeems your life from the pit
>> and crowns you with love and compassion,
> who satisfies your desires with good things
>> so that your youth is renewed like the eagle's.
>
> (Ps. 103:1–5)

THIRTEEN

Living in Freedom

Juggling school and work after getting settled in Phoenix, I was grateful my parents had made the move with me. While my mother continued to be critical at times of my parenting skills, she and Dad were a big help taking care of Chris. They encouraged me to put my best foot forward with this opportunity for a fresh start. It helped that we quickly found a church that focused on the power of the Holy Spirit in our lives, and I was hopeful that we would find the same sweet fellowship we'd had with our church community back in Texas.

Despite growing stronger spiritually, I was still feeling disoriented by the move and the new adult steps I was taking. Motherhood drained me physically and emotionally, and part of me was still reeling from running into Kyle right before we had moved. He and I were polite if not a bit awkward at first, and he asked if we could go somewhere and talk. I agreed to meet him later that day at a local park, knowing it might be my last time ever to see him. Though I did not want to be in a relationship with him, he still stirred up so many old emotions in me. And, of course, he was the father of my beautiful baby boy.

I still couldn't fathom how he could just walk away from his own flesh and blood, from the responsibility he had fathered through the consequences of his actions. I even decided to bring Chris with me, thinking that if Kyle saw his adorable son that it would melt his heart. So as I drove to the park that day, I prayed that God would give me strength and provide a clear indication of whether Kyle could be part of our baby's future. If Kyle could see his son and still walk away, I knew it was indeed time to sever any lingering ties and move on with my life.

With the late afternoon sunshine filtering through rows of cumulus clouds, we pushed the stroller through the park until we came to a bench beneath the shade of a gazebo. Kyle commented on how cute the baby was, but that was about it. Staring down at his son, he might as well have been looking at a friend's new puppy. As Chris dozed, Kyle and I sipped water bottles, and I accepted the fact that Kyle would not be a presence in our baby's life.

"You look good," Kyle said. "I guess motherhood agrees with you."

"Thanks," I said. "He's a good baby. Plus Mom and Dad help."

I could sense he had something he wanted to say, but I didn't feel I should have to help him say it. So we sat there in silence for a few moments.

"Listen, Tam," he finally said. "I'm sorry about . . . how all this turned out. But I'm not ready to settle down. I leave for Dallas this weekend to start school."

"I know. And I wish you well."

He nodded. "My dad—you know how he is—he's worried about . . . he wants you to sign some papers the lawyer dropped off. It basically says that I'm not your baby's father and won't have to pay you child support or anything like that."

"Really?" I said. "You think I'd do that? Come after you and force you to take responsibility for your own son?"

He stood up and shook his head. "Don't be like that, okay? This is hard enough."

I laughed and stood up, too, so I could face him. "This has been hard on *you*? I'm so sorry for you—I really am. But you don't have a clue."

Kyle's green eyes flashed with anger, but he held his tongue.

"I'll sign whatever your parents want me to sign," I said. "As long as it also terminates any rights you have to be involved in my son's life. It goes both ways, Kyle."

"Fair enough," he said. "Don't worry—I'm not going to . . . like I said, I'm just not ready to settle down."

Chris roused in the stroller, and I wondered if he was getting too hot.

"We need to go," I said. "Anything else?"

Kyle shook his head, looking sad for the first time that visit.

"I wish you the best, Kyle," I said. "I really do."

I took the handle of the stroller, began pushing it gently, and walked away.

He sat down with his head in his hands.

Though I had peace about how things were between us, I still felt sad.

———

With the paperwork signed terminating any legal paternity rights Kyle had to our son, I felt free to move on and begin my new life in Phoenix. Our new church was welcoming, but I didn't have much time to make friends. Plus, I felt self-conscious as a young, single mother. Part of this might have been the vibe I sensed from Mom and Dad, perhaps some lingering shame they felt, as if my status reflected back on them. Consequently, I began to feel the old pangs of loneliness that used to send me out with friends or into Kyle's arms. Without those default resources to run to, I was forced to rely on God more than ever.

One morning while I was praying, I came to a new realization that lifted even more of the emotional weight of the past off my shoulders. The Holy Spirit faithfully provided the revelation that helped me break free from the oppression I had suffered for so many years. That morning I sat in a rocking chair beside the window with Chris asleep in my arms after his breakfast. Suddenly I heard a quiet voice deep within me, the whisper of God's Spirit, gently ask, *Tamara, are you my servant?*

Yes, Lord, I replied.

Then why do you continue trying to serve two masters when you know you can have only one? You are my child and I will take care of you. Leave the past behind you. I will make all things new again.

Tears trickled down my face as I nodded and agreed. In that moment I saw a flashback of the past few years of my life and how I had consistently divided my heart and run to other people instead of my heavenly Father. Like a needle stuck in the same groove of an old record, I would walk in obedience as faithfully as I could, trusting God to fill the void in my life. Then I would reach a point where I wondered why the void still ached within my heart until I would begin to look for comfort and consolation from other people. Little by little I would slip back into giving them the power to determine how I felt and whether I thought I was okay or not. Eventually, however, I would reach a point of turmoil that I couldn't handle, and it would cause me to repent. Once again, I'd live for God and rely solely on him until I began to allow my emotions to derail my thoughts and actions. Then I'd take ownership for filling the void my own way, in my own time.

This cycle had repeated itself over and over.

But now I sensed I would finally break free.

"Lord," I prayed that morning, "I see the cycle I've been caught up in for years, the same one that I've asked you to break, and yet I still struggle. Why do you withhold your healing touch from my heart? I know you can fill this emptiness inside me and meet all my needs, so why do I continue to wrestle so hard? Won't I ever be free? Won't I ever be able to help deliver others from this bondage just as you delivered me from the pain of hell? All I need is one touch to be whole. Please do not withhold your hand."

I placed Chris down in his crib, where he continued sleeping. I knelt by my bed, tears running down my face. Feeling so broken and empty, I couldn't understand why I tried so hard and yet continued to fall short.

Then the Holy Spirit revealed the reason. God told me he had been waiting on me to surrender my disobedience and idolatry before him, acknowledging my ongoing attempts to always fill the void inside by my own efforts. He wanted my whole heart, not just 98 percent of it. He was waiting for me to make the decision to obey him *even if my emotional needs went unmet.*

In that moment I saw clearly how I withheld certain parts of my heart, willing to serve God in those areas only if he filled me and healed me the way I thought he should. Because he hadn't come through the way I wanted and expected, I felt justified in finding a way to meet my own desires. Bottom line: I was serving myself more than I was serving him.

With another outpouring of tears, I opened my heart and repented. I committed to put God first regardless of how I felt or if my needs were ever met the way I longed for. I made the choice to surrender my control and to end my own attempts at serving myself. I was through yo-yo-ing back and forth, up and down when I knew the absolute truth of who God was and what he had done in my life—and what he longs to do in the lives of all his children.

As I rose from my knees, I sensed a fresh immersion in God's Spirit, and my heart filled with peace. I could actually feel more healing taking place in my soul, like the tingling sensation of antiseptic over a cut. I knew I would still struggle at times—and I have—but I also knew God was faithful and would continue to minister to me and meet my needs according to his divine wisdom—not the urgency or volatility of my emotions. The Bible promises us, "He will also keep you firm to the end, so that you will be blameless on the day of our Lord Jesus Christ. God is faithful, who has called you into fellowship with his Son, Jesus Christ our Lord" (1 Cor. 1:8–9). I knew it to be true.

—

Making the decision to be obedient, even if my emotional needs were never met, was not an easy one. I would have to learn to trust God at a deeper level and have complete faith in his Spirit's ability to take care of me regardless of circumstances and my changing emotions. I was discovering the reality of putting God first and allowing him to abide in me as the center of my life.

God wants his presence to engulf us hourly, daily, yet so often we push him away by our unwillingness to relinquish control of meeting our own needs. We are so opposed to any kind of pain, discomfort, or inconvenience that we get in our own way. When we let go of trying to serve ourselves, we give God room to work in us and through us. But this process does require patience and suffering. It requires trusting God and his perfect timing instead of always chasing after a fix for ourselves.

As I've grown older and watched our society become dependent on technology, I worry that we've become conditioned toward self-reliance and instant gratification even more. We think we can have virtually anything our heart desires with only a click, snap, or tweet, but we can't trust ourselves or any man-made device more than we can trust God.

Abiding in Jesus means remaining reliant on him as we persevere in our faith and follow him each day. We must commit to our relationship with him no matter what happens—even when the worst, the unthinkable, the unimaginable occurs. We must endure and trust in his ability to sustain us beyond what we think we're able to bear, cleaving to God's Word and keeping our focus on him—and on our purpose of loving and serving others, choosing to walk in complete forgiveness of all offense.

For so much of my life up to that point, I had focused only on how I felt. I continually let myself be pulled down into the undertow of pain, disappointment, heartache, and loss swirling around inside me. How could I remain centered on God when I allowed my moods to be the driving force for my actions? I realized how one-sided my style of relating to God had been—even after all he had done for me in rescuing me from hell, forgiving my sins, and restoring me to new life.

My heart was grieved that day to realize how selfish I had been when I was willing to do what God asked of me only if I felt like it. Otherwise, I was off the hook, feeling too broken, too fragile, too wounded to obey and trust him. I would reach out and minister to others if the conditions were right. But most of the time my priority was myself, feeling happy, being whole, and not having to go without the love, approval, and affirmation I so desperately craved.

It's funny, but I realized how I would feel if I were in God's place in our relationship. How would I feel if a good friend only came around to ask for money to pay off her debts? Time after time, she wouldn't want to spend time together to get to know me and invest in our friendship—she would simply be there to see what she could get out of me. How would I feel if this friend only talked about her problems and her feelings and her heartaches all the time? What if she never asked about how I felt or what I thought? Simply put, I would feel used.

Relationships are always a two-way street, a collaborative partnership requiring communication, understanding, and revelation in order to build and sustain intimacy. God desires a relationship with all of us because we are his children, created in his image. Though he lacks absolutely nothing, he wants his people to worship him and to invite him into their lives so they can become a reflection and extension of his love.

Our hearts, when dependent on Christ, are then free to give compassion to all those around us. We can show mercy to the hurting because of the mercy we have been given so freely. We can facilitate God's healing because of what we have experienced of his Spirit's work in our broken hearts. We can serve the needs of others by becoming the hands and feet of Jesus. As we walk with the Lord, our priorities shift from our own needs to the needs of others. Our priorities become centered on God as we speak and to show his love to the world around us. As Jesus said, "By this everyone will know that you are my disciples, if you love one another" (John 13:35).

It was a spoonful of good medicine to realize I was responsible to find out what God's Word said about my situation and in doing so purposefully renew my mind. I keenly desired to place my heart in a position of forgiveness and to walk in understanding of and compassion for others when they did things to hurt me. My goal is to honor God in everything I do, submitting my mind and emotions to the Holy Spirit.

Maybe motherhood had something to do with it. Maybe it was moving to Phoenix. Or maybe it was just the reality of finally growing up. But most assuredly, it was the Holy Spirit working and moving in my heart. Regardless of the combination of factors influencing me, I knew without a doubt that God was changing me.

———

I moved and lived in a few other states with Mom and Dad for a few years before sensing God was leading me to a job back in Texas. By that time I was feeling a little restless and eager to move on with my life without feeling so dependent on my parents. I also sensed that they needed more time for themselves and were homesick for Texas. While they would never leave me and Chris, I wanted to let them know that I was ready to be entirely on my own.

I had continued to share my story whenever given an opportunity or prompted by the Spirit. When I spoke in front of the youth group at our church in Arizona, the response was similar to the one back home in Texas. Many young people related to the emotional battle with rejection and the longing to fit in. They understood why I became so despondent that I was willing to end my life rather than continue to struggle in pain. And they were riveted by my description of hell and heaven and the utter joy and wholeness I felt in the presence of God. So many of them accepted the Lord into their hearts that night, and I was blessed by simply knowing I was God's instrument. I was doing what he had saved me to do.

There were still struggles, of course, as I worried about what people thought of me, aware that some discounted me because I was a single mom. Others may have dismissed me because of my youth or because my experience did not fit into their understanding of Scripture or their particular theology. But I never let criticism deter me from giving others a glimpse into my soul and the eternity-altering experience I had endured.

My heart's desire then, as it remains now, was to share with others the love of our magnificent, almighty God. His love is truly perfect and conquers all obstacles, barriers, problems, and weaknesses. As Paul wrote, "I am convinced that neither death nor life, neither angels nor demons, neither the present nor the future, nor any powers, neither height nor depth, nor anything else in all creation, will be able to separate us from the love of God that is in Christ Jesus our Lord" (Rom. 8:38–39).

It's so tempting to think we're unworthy of God's love because of all the mistakes we've made, all the bad choices and sinful habits with which we continue to struggle. We feel so undeserving of forgiveness, often unwilling to forgive ourselves even after we know God has washed us clean through the blood Jesus shed for us on the cross. Or perhaps we feel that God is too far away, too far removed from the ins and outs of our lives each day to really care about us and be involved in our lives.

We easily feel overwhelmed by the thought that we're one small speck in a great big world. We ask, why are we worthy of God's time and attention? Most of all, we may wonder, as I did for so many years, why we have gone through so much suffering if God does indeed really love us.

I certainly don't have all the answers, but I do know that our suffering results from two factors—the gift to freely choose whom we will serve and the consequences of sin from our original parents, Adam and Eve. The Enemy planted seeds of disobedience in their minds, and they allowed them to take root and blossom into the stain of sin that would be passed down to all their offspring—all except one, Jesus. The familiar truth found in John 3:16 reflects the sacrifice our heavenly Father made by sending his only Son to earth to live and die as a man so we could enjoy restoration, redemption, and relationship with him forever.

The foundation of our human suffering is sin and disobedience, selfishness and idolatry. But the Savior we have is more powerful! Once again, Paul expresses this so well in his letter to the church in Rome: "Oh, what a miserable person I am! Who will free me from this life that is dominated by sin and death? Thank God! The answer is in Jesus Christ our Lord" (Rom. 7:24–25 NLT). Our Savior waits patiently for us to come to him with our broken pieces and allow his Spirit to live in us and transform us into his likeness, complete wholeness and holy perfection.

The only way we can live in the freedom we have in Christ's victory is through the indwelling of the Holy Spirit. Powered by the Spirit, we must claim the authority we have over sin in our lives. During this season of my life, I learned to practice this directly.

When I felt afraid and anxious, I would command fear to leave my mind, body, and emotions in the name of Jesus

Christ and through the power of his resurrection. If the Enemy tried to use my loneliness as leverage to tempt me, I would pray and overcome any power my feelings had by the ultimate power of the blood of Jesus. I would bind those fears and destructive desires and release the love of God in my life instead.

If we don't claim and exercise this spiritual authority, we continue to suffer. It's like living in a jail cell even though Jesus has unlocked the door and loosed the chains that once held us captive. We're free, but we must leave the bars and chains behind and walk in the liberty of his love. God's Word tells us, "It is for freedom that Christ has set us free. Stand firm, then, and do not let yourselves be burdened again by a yoke of slavery" (Gal. 5:1).

The choice is yours.

Freedom or fear.

Life or death.

Which will it be?

FOURTEEN

Moving and Growing

Moving is always a mixed blessing. At first there's the excitement of a new beginning, a fresh start, and the promise of what the Lord has for you in this place where he has led you. On the other hand, there's also the fear of the unknown, the anxious edge of unfamiliarity, and the loneliness of not knowing anyone and having to start building relationships all over again. Nonetheless, I never regretted leaving Arizona and following the Lord to a new venture in Tennessee.

And this move was definitely orchestrated by God. One Sunday at lunch in Arizona, as we partook of Mom's delicious Southern cooking, I began to share that I felt we should move east—not East Coast east but somewhere in the Southeast perhaps. Mom piped in on how the Lord had been speaking to her heart, and she agreed it was time for a change. One of my siblings was visiting, and she and her husband said they had been talking about moving as well. It was as if God had been speaking to each of us individually before bringing us together at that table to confirm that it was time to move together.

Dad pulled out his old paper atlas and unfolded it like a giant napkin. We all prayed and asked the Holy Spirit to direct our steps into his perfect will. The six of us laughed and talked about all the beautiful places we might like to reside. Looking at the map, our focus landed on Tennessee, and we agreed it was exactly where we were supposed to go. We knew it had to be the Lord leading us to the Volunteer State, since we had never been there before. When my sister and her spouse put in a job transfer request that was accepted immediately, it was further confirmation. So we all resigned from our obligations, packed up everything we owned, and moved to a new home not far from Nashville.

Through prayer, God quickly led us to a strong, Bible-based church focused on living by the power of the Holy Spirit, and that certainly helped us settle in. Our brothers and sisters in Christ there were quick to embrace my son and me into their community and help us begin our new life.

But I'll be honest—I struggled more than I thought I would. No matter how strong your faith or how closely you walk with the Lord, the realities of being a single parent keep you humble. Finding a Christian preschool for Chris— that I could afford—proved harder than I expected. So when Mom insisted she was willing to make the sacrifices to care for him, I was beyond grateful.

My new job was exciting at first, but then the realities that you find in any workplace set in: office politics, corporate bureaucracy, and the tendency to gossip about other coworkers.

I knew I was where God wanted me to be, but I had naïvely assumed my life would therefore be easier. In many ways, it was just the opposite, a truth that would be reinforced each time I moved or experienced a major change in my life as the result of following God. Relocating to Tennessee, I had to realize that he was calling us to our next destination so we could relax and be on vacation, but so he could continue to strengthen our faith even as he used us for his kingdom purposes in the lives of others. It wasn't easy working, going to school, taking care of my active toddler, and trying to take care of myself in healthy ways too.

No surprise, then, that old fears began to creep into my thinking. *You'll never fit in here,* I'd think. *Others judge you because you have a son and aren't married. Everyone here already has a community of family and friends—they don't need you. You're an outsider. You always have been, and you always will be. And as far as meeting a man after God's own heart? No good Christian man will ever want you. Not after all you've been through.*

I knew the Enemy was preying on my weakness and trying to undermine my faith in God to meet my needs. And even though I worked hard to take such false, negative thoughts captive to Christ, I found the battle exhausting. But God was faithful to sustain me, giving me new, fresh mercies each day. Not a day went by when I didn't pray the promise of Philippians 4:13 (KJV), "I can do all things through Christ which strengtheneth me," at least once.

During this season of my life, the emphasis was definitely on "all things." Just as I began feeling settled in my new life in Tennessee, I felt the Lord calling me to move again, this time to Arkansas. Relocating would not only provide further job opportunities and a better education, but it would show my willingness to be sensitive to his leading. Finally, I would be out on my own, just me and my son, without the safety net of my parents and family. I was nervous but knew this was a faith-stretching opportunity. I would have to depend on God more than ever.

Looking for a job in Arkansas, I encountered many unforeseen challenges. I had already witnessed firsthand the bias against promoting women in the workplace, especially mothers, because of the assumption that they were not as committed and hardworking as their male counterparts. More important, however, after praying and fasting, I sensed the Holy Spirit guiding me to accept yet another major change looming ahead.

While I enjoyed Arkansas and felt more at home there than any of the other places I'd lived since leaving Texas, I soon found myself being recruited for a job in Houston. The frequent moves were starting to wear on me, and since Chris was getting older, I wanted something more permanent. This new position in Houston seemed to fit the bill, offering the familiarity of Texas with the appeal of a major big city. I knew it would be challenging, but as I began to see the big three-O looming on the birthday horizon, I knew it was a risk the Lord was leading me to take.

Little did I know what—and who—God had in store for me there.

———

"What's a nice girl like you doing in a place like this?"

I giggled and smiled at my new coworker, Rodney, who shook my hand and listened as I described how I had come to work in our company's Houston office. He was a striking man with brown hair, sparkling eyes, and a natural charisma that immediately put me at ease. As I moved on to the rest of my orientation and introductions, he lingered in my mind, but I wasn't sure why. A brief thought whispered that he would become my future mate. But the last thing I had on my agenda was dating and marriage. My fleeting thought left me wondering if it was divinely inspired, the longing of my heart, or both.

While the move and new job seemed to be going smoothly on the surface, I churned with angry emotions inside. The many moves in a short period of time were taking a toll. Despite making advancement in my career, I still struggled to make ends meet and lived paycheck to paycheck. I had no real lasting friends because I had moved so frequently, and even when guys from work or church asked me out, I continually turned them down. I used work or not having a sitter as my excuses, but I knew the real reason.

I was afraid of men and the power I seemed to give them to validate me. I wanted to be strong in the Lord and depend only on him, and I feared that allowing myself to be attracted to and loved by a man would only set me up for emotional disaster. Wounded by the collateral damage of my parents' divorce in childhood, I knew how painful any relationship could be.

Scarred from the past, I became angry because the longing for a godly man in my life lingered. As much as I didn't want to admit it, I secretly wanted to find a man I could build a life with, a good-hearted man who loved the Lord and shared the same values and dreams that I held so dear. I wanted a man who would not only be my husband and love me the way Christ loves the church, but who would also naturally love and accept Chris as his son.

By the time I started that new job in Houston, however, I was pretty sure no such man existed. And that made me angry at God in ways I had never experienced before. I knew it wasn't rational, and I truly believed he had a plan for my life filled with good things and the abundance of his blessings. But he sure did seem to be taking his sweet time about revealing any of it to me. How long was I going to have to scrape by financially? How long would I be alone raising my little boy?

As it turned out, not long at all.

———

Fast-forward several months later, and I'm sitting with Rodney in a very nice restaurant enjoying a glass of wine. It's not a date, but more an unspoken matter of emotional convenience for us both. The spark of connection I had felt with him the first time we met allowed us to work well together and to become friends quickly. He was going through a painful divorce, one he had resisted at first, and trying to figure out what he wanted out of life. Only a year earlier, he thought he had life figured out—wife, career, new home, all the things our culture tells us we need. But now his life was unraveling.

Raised in a Catholic family, Rodney visited a Baptist church with a friend while in high school and committed his life to the Lord there. Rodney's initial burst of excitement over his new faith quickly flared out, though, without the support of others in his life. God never intended his children to walk alone. Without family and friends to encourage him, to instruct him, and to disciple him in the ways of God, Rodney slipped back into the way he had been living before giving his heart to Jesus. He married someone he thought he loved, he worked hard to get ahead, and yet his life seemed so empty.

While I knew I shouldn't be drinking alcohol in the company of a man who was legally still married, I was so lonely I couldn't resist the opportunity to enjoy a real friendship with someone who was willing to reveal his heart to me. Consequently, he and I began to support and encourage each other, sometimes enjoying a drink together, and then once his divorce was final, actually enjoying dinner together or taking Chris to the park. He was easy to talk to and we had so much in common. He liked me without any ulterior motive or selfish expectation.

Our friendship continued to blossom, and Rodney and I were married four years later. During the time leading up to our wedding, we became the best of friends. Rodney experienced a revival of faith in his life as he renewed his commitment to Jesus and invited the Holy Spirit to dwell inside him. He not only accepted Chris but loved him as his own son even though coming together as a family wasn't always easy. Rodney accepted the baggage of my past without ever judging me or doubting me in any way. I confided in him about all my issues with my parents, including my biological father, as well as the sibling rivalry that remained a part of our family's current dynamic.

Rodney shared about his own family background and the struggle he had faced growing up. He opened his heart to me and displayed an integrity and honesty I had not encountered in another man before. He was different and delighted in my company for no good reason other than he loved me. We complemented each other in so many ways and were companions to each other in our spiritual journeys. Not surprisingly, each of us could see the way God had been working in the other's life all along, visible in ways that we ourselves could not see with such clarity.

God had brought us together, and I continue to thank him every day for my husband. Rodney is my rock and always points me back to God. We are blessed to have two daughters—each a miracle after I had been told by doctors that I could not conceive again. He is such an amazing father, so loving and supportive in ways I never experienced with my father while growing up. Perhaps best of all, Rodney and I have the privilege of ministering together.

Through a variety of trials and triumphs—I'll save those for my next book!—we have seen God work in people's lives in the most humbling and dramatic ways. My husband and I have witnessed miracles of physical and emotional healing. We have seen God heal the scars of childhood abuse as relationships are healed and families are mended. We have seen God provide food, water, and medicine for impoverished people both in our community in Houston and in communities around the world.

I am so blessed to have Rodney for my husband. God knew the kind of man I needed in my life, and he is far better than I could ever have chosen for myself. When I look back now at all the anger, loneliness, and heartache I experienced for that first decade of my adult life, I can see how God was preparing me to be the best woman of faith, wife, and mother I could be. I'm still far from perfect, a pilgrim of grace just like you. But I'm a little wiser, a tiny bit more patient, and a whole lot more grateful for the loving presence of God in my life.

———

One of the many gifts Rodney has given me is encouragement to tell my story.

While some men might be ashamed or intimidated by the dramatic testimony of my after-death experience and the years that followed, he celebrates it as evidence of God's love, grace, mercy, and power. My husband has always viewed me as his equal, his partner, even as he leads our family with the sacrificial strength and servant leadership God outlines for husbands in Scripture. Rodney is not intimidated by my strength or by the depth of my sensitivity and the power of my emotions. He views them as precious gifts God has given me so I can know the pain of others and show them the same compassionate love Jesus has shown me.

Rodney even encouraged me to share my testimony in written form, unsurprised when I told him that I felt God's Spirit compelling me to write a book. During my many moves, I had lost the written account of all I had experienced in hell and heaven that Pastor Bob had counseled me to write and keep, but I still recalled it with vivid clarity. With Rodney's encouragement and the power of the Holy Spirit, I wrote and published my first book, *Delivered: A Death-Defying Journey into Heaven and Hell*, back in 2006.

As painful as it was to share my life in writing, I know God has used it in many people's lives, reminding them of the spiritual realities they will face after their life on earth ends. I was even interviewed by Pat Robertson on *The 700 Club* and invited back for a follow-up interview after such a large outpouring of viewer interest. My book led to speaking invitations and served as a catalyst for ministry in so many churches, schools, orphanages, and hospitals around the world.

There was a backlash, of course, because there will always be persecution for those who preach the truth of the gospel and the power of Christ's blood to save sinners. But the blessings that have come from that book continue to this day—to this very book you are reading right now. Why another book focused on the same major event in my life? Why now?

There are many reasons, but please allow me to share a few important ones. When I wrote *Delivered*, I mostly focused on spiritual life and the liberation I experienced after my visit to hell and heaven. Reading it now, I'm amazed at how little I actually describe my life experience, focusing instead on the truth of Scripture and its impact on my healing and maturation. Both are essential, of course, and after *Delivered* came out, I had always hoped that I might have another opportunity to write about my testimony, this time focusing more on the details of my story, because that is often what people tell me they relate to the most.

In the perfect timing of the Lord, I was given that opportunity when a publisher approached me about telling my story again in a new book. The result is now in your hands! I like to think of these two books as different sides to the same life-changing coin, complementing and enhancing each other in my attempt to honor the calling God placed on my life when he delivered me from hell and restored me to life.

———

Death is truly a humbling experience, to say the least. It's sobering to see what your eternal future—and everyone else's—holds. My after-death experience has definitely taught me to practice humility and to extend compassion on a regular basis. I must search my heart with courage to see where my morals and values stand. I can't base my morals or values on my surroundings or my feelings, but must base them on the principles of the Most High God. I have learned not to compare myself with others, but instead to simply be open and honest with a willingness to be transparent before God.

As I have matured in my walk with Christ, I have learned that every time I get tempted to go astray, I must double-check my heart to see if I am completely trusting God. I have realized that when I want only temporary pleasures, my focus is on me—and I fall short every time. Yet, when I look past my immediate comfort and look at the greater picture, I enable the Holy Spirit to keep my focus on God—and victory always follows.

I must always remember to prepare myself daily for the moment when I meet my heavenly Father face-to-face. Jesus has taught me that I must be honest with myself first before I can be honest with God, or anyone else for that matter. Being honest with my thoughts, feelings, actions and responses has brought me closer to the Lord. The more open I am about my own faults, the less I throw stones at someone else.

Judging others keeps us from receiving God's grace, for we will be judged in the same manner in which we judge others. In my life I can't afford judgment because I am guilty and need only mercy and grace to abound in my life, not judgment. Too often, we judge others in order to justify ourselves and our opinions. But this only fuels selfishness, sinfulness, and idolatry!

We must therefore lay down our judgments, opinions, and comparisons to others at the feet of Jesus. We must ask him to transform them. We must leave the judging to him and not the limitations and selfishness of our human hearts. We must remember the admonition against judging that Jesus himself gave us:

> "Do not judge, or you too will be judged. For in the same way you judge others, you will be judged, and with the measure you use, it will be measured to you.
>
> "Why do you look at the speck of sawdust in your brother's eye and pay no attention to the plank in your own eye? How can you say to your brother, 'Let me take the speck out of your eye,' when all the time there is a plank in your own eye? You hypocrite, first take the plank out of your own eye, and then you will see clearly to remove the speck from your brother's eye." (Matt. 7:1–5)

How can we resolve our own issues if we continue to blame others for our struggles? Just because someone mistreats us doesn't give us the right to feel and act any way we choose. It only gives us the opportunity to forgive and to show grace. All of us have flaws and character defects, and each one of us must focus on working out our own salvation with fear and trembling (Phil. 2:12). We must know we serve a mighty God who is the only true and just God. The Word teaches that to be the greatest is to become the least. We must let go of our attitudes of anger, resentment, and self-righteousness.

Can you relate to what I'm saying, dear friend?

The choice is yours.

You must take responsibility for yourself, for your life, for whom you are serving. You're either serving God, fallen angels, or yourself. You must realize the ultimate reality, the consequences of your choices. Now is the time you must choose where you will spend eternity.

Right now—before it's too late!

FIFTEEN

We All Need
Second Chances

Even after all these years, I can still feel the intensely vivid sensations of my out-of-body journey. The rush of falling, sheer-off-a-cliff falling, only moments after the .38-caliber bullet pierced my body. Being swallowed by darkness into an all-consuming, scorching acid bath, drenching every atom of my being with misery. Aching with a pain so vibrant and unrelenting. Knowing I was fully separated from life, from light, from all that is good and holy—for the rest of eternity.

When you think of hell, you probably conjure up images of fire and imagine the kind of heat you feel when you burn your finger. But this is so inadequate compared to the very real place! A third-degree burn would feel like a gentle touch compared to the sensation I experienced in that dreadful place of torment. And it's so much more than a feeling or sensation, because you actually become the essence of sin. You turn into a being of death, a lifeless soul cut off from the only source of life, Jesus Christ.

When I experienced hell there was utter darkness, a pure, black void where light was completely absent. The reason it was so dark was that Jesus was not present there. Jesus is the source of Light. In fact, he told us as much: "I am the light of the world. Whoever follows me will never walk in darkness, but will have the light of life" (John 8:12).

Based on my visit to hell, I have a clear understanding and distinct appreciation of this declaration. In hell, the place where I first landed after death, Jesus was nowhere to be found. The void of his absence was the most painful reality I've ever encountered. There was no light at all, only pure and abysmal darkness. Empty. Hollow. The essence of darkness distilled into one place.

It makes sense, really. Life equals light and death equals darkness. The first thing God did to begin creation was separate the light from the darkness. God knew light would nourish and sustain the new life he was creating—plants, animals, people. In addition to growth for new life, light would provide warmth and illumination.

No wonder Jesus Christ is the ultimate Light and the source of our redemption. Through the blood sacrifice of the Lamb that was slain on Calvary, you and I can enter into this Light. We can see with an eternal perspective, penetrating the darkness around us on earth and looking beyond where we are toward our spiritual home in heaven. We can experience new life as we are transformed into the image of Jesus. We can reflect the warmth and life-giving power he offers to all people.

Light or dark—it's that simple. You may feel overwhelmed by trying to understand what lies ahead for you in eternity. You might feel confused by my account if you're comparing it with others you've read. But there's really only one thing you need to understand. *Heaven and hell are real, and you choose where you will go and what you will become.* God gives you a choice even as he continues to reveal himself to you in so many ways.

Please understand: I chose hell because I had not made Jesus the Lord of my life. Ultimately, how you die is not important, but the condition of your soul in that moment when it leaves your earthly body matters more than you may realize. I'm aware others have died physically and say they visited hell, saw heaven, or met Jesus. I cannot speak for them or assess what they experienced. I don't know the status of their souls or where they will end up when they die again. Only God knows in the vast wisdom of a holy, just judge and a compassionate, merciful redeemer.

But what I do know is that we all must choose and live out the path revealed by our choice. You see, there's a difference between believing that Jesus exists or that he is who he said he is—the Son of God, the Messiah, the Prince of Peace, and the Savior of us all. You have to choose to go one step further and make him Lord of your life. You have to respond to your belief and act on it.

———

My dear friend, have you begun to grasp what I'm compelled to share with you? Can you embrace the personal relevance this amazing reality has for your own life? Can you possibly comprehend the magnitude of this truth? The absolute truth of eternal damnation is real and does exist after you leave this earth. I don't know any other way to say it—plain and simple. It sounds harsh and unpleasant but not nearly as unbearable as being cut off from God for eternity in the anguish of hell.

Sometimes I feel so frustrated when I share my testimony with others because I ultimately cannot convince them or make the decision that will determine their destiny for them. I don't know how to make spiritual matters understandable for mortal minds or describe eternal realities in temporal terms. I relate to the Scripture where Jesus says, "I have spoken to you of earthly things and you do not believe; how then will you believe if I speak of heavenly things?" (John 3:12).

Ultimately, it's not up to me—where you spend eternity is up to *you.*

God's Word plainly tells us about our future, yet our own self-righteous attitudes often block our comprehension that judgment will happen to us just as it will happen for every human soul. Some people perpetuate their delusion that God is too good to send us to hell. But you must realize that we send ourselves there—against God's relentless pursuit to redeem and rescue us. He's not trying to punish us—he loves us like a strong, gentle Father who holds us close and protects us from the Enemy and the weakness within ourselves.

Just as parents set rules in place for their children, so our heavenly Father gives us rules for our own benefit. Many of us say with our mouths that we love God more than anything else, yet our daily routines have nothing to do with him. Just because we go to church and pray before meals doesn't mean we love God with all our hearts. We must look inward to discover our actual motive for the things we do and our purposes for living every moment.

Excuses won't cut it when we stand face-to-face with our Creator. As sure as you were born, you will stand before the righteous Judge. It isn't about what you do *for* God—it's about knowing and loving him. You can spend your lifetime doing charitable works and serving others—but why and who you're doing it for matters more. Jesus told us, "Not everyone who says to me, 'Lord, Lord,' will enter the kingdom of heaven, but only the one who does the will of my Father who is in heaven. Many will say to me on that day, 'Lord, Lord, did we not prophesy in your name and in your name drive out demons and in your name perform many miracles?' Then I will tell them plainly, 'I never knew you. Away from me, you evildoers!'" (Matt. 7:21–23).

So often we spend our time, energy, and resources on

chasing something for personal gain. Even when we try to focus on others and give charitably, we're often doing it with the mixed motive of feeling good about ourselves. Now, it's good to give even when our motives may not be pure. God often uses us despite ourselves. But one day our motives will be revealed and like the physical condition of our bodies, those motives will indicate our spiritual health.

We can never do enough or give enough—and thank God for the gift of his Son, Jesus, because we don't have to. We are enough simply by being his children. By faith we choose to receive salvation and by God's binding love we are able to have a relationship with him. He gives us the gift of his Holy Spirit as our friend, companion, and guide.

Our actions reflect our relationships as well as who we are individually. When you have a close relationship with Jesus, the quality of your relationship emerges just as it does in a good marriage. When husband and wife influence each other and begin to share a life as one, they create something better than they were as individuals. When Jesus is a part of your life, the Light of God shines through for all to see.

You can live in the light.

Or you can hide in the dark.

But you must choose now where you will be later.

———

As our time together comes to a close, I pray you will heed all I have shared with you. We all make mistakes and we all need second chances, so consider this a wake-up call from God. Don't go back to sleep, hitting snooze to silence the voice of the Holy Spirit. Remain awake to the reality of God's presence in your life.

If nothing else, please know there are eternal consequences to every decision you make! To live means to be in the presence of the Lord, and to die means to be separated from God's presence. There is a physical death, which is the separation of the soul from the body, and then there is a second death, which is an eternal separation of the unbeliever from God in the lake of fire. From his throne in heaven, Christ declares:

> "I am the Alpha and the Omega, the Beginning and the End. To the thirsty I will give water without cost from the spring of the water of life. Those who are victorious will inherit all this, and I will be their God and they will be my children. But the cowardly, the unbelieving, the vile, the murderers, the sexually immoral, those who practice magic arts, the idolaters and all liars—they will be consigned to the fiery lake of burning sulfur. This is the second death." (Rev. 21:6–8)

I pray you are making the right decision: the decision to live covered by the blood of Jesus. This is the very reason Jesus died on the cross. His love for us is so great that he doesn't want us to be banished from him forever. He desires a relationship with each and every one of us, yet we often turn away from our relationship with him because it is easy to blame him for our problems and run from the truth. Our Enemy encourages us to focus on our problems and inadequacies instead of on the hope and love of God.

It is our Enemy's goal to separate us from God, and he is always lurking over our shoulders to condemn us for the mistakes we make. If we could only realize the mercy and grace God gives to us no matter how many times we mess up.

I know that for some of you it is difficult to believe what I am saying. You may think that if you completely accept what I say as the truth, this would require change on your part, and you're not ready to make any changes. Possibly it's just hard to accept that there are consequences to our sins. God tells us how to escape destruction, but most of us are just too stubborn to listen. Jesus said, "I am the way and the truth and the life. No one comes to the Father except through me" (John 14:6).

Please, I beg you to listen to this warning! Hell is real, and I experienced it. Every second you delay in bowing down before almighty God is one you can't afford to waste. You aren't guaranteed another second in this life, because God owes you nothing, yet you owe him everything. Jesus paid a debt he did not owe, and we owe a debt we cannot pay. The Bible makes it clear. Every knee will bow and every tongue will confess Jesus as Lord (Phil. 2:9–11).

The question is this: Will you do it now and live your life serving him, or will you be stubborn, believing you know what's best for your own life and have plenty of time to do it later? If "later" is in your heart, you might end up confessing with great sorrow. If "later" never comes, there won't be any way for you to turn back and change the eternal decision you have made once this life is over.

Sin grows and takes root so gradually in our hearts. Once you lie, steal, cheat, or commit any other sin, it gets easier each time you give in to it. Whatever you feed your mind and heart is eventually what you will become. You must be careful and deliberate about the "soul food" you take in. For instance, we're conditioned and influenced by media, advertisers, and the entertainment world about how we dress, the things we buy, the reputation we want to have, and how we live our lives. But the Enemy knows how to use this cultural pressure as a crowbar along the fractures in our lives. He uses it to play on our fears and insecurities, our longings and desires, our doubts and disappointments. But we must see beyond life today to life in eternity.

This life is just the beginning, and yet the way we live it will determine everything in our eternal future. Eternity is such a large, intangible concept that we tend to dismiss it. But it's essential to understand eternity in the context of how we exist from now until our souls leave our mortal bodies behind. God created us to be eternal beings in temporary bodies. The way you choose to live your life will determine whether or not you turn into sin or become love for eternity.

Too many people focus on their problems or on pleasing or manipulating their relationships with others to get what they think they want. But this only leads to death.

Instead, turn your eyes to God, not to people, because focusing on others will keep you from God's best and possibly even from eternal life. So many people in church believe but don't act on their beliefs. Hypocrisy is a problem both inside and outside the church because people don't always follow through with what they know is right. Each of us is responsible for our own personal relationship with God, and without that relationship you will only suffer.

Why would you want to continue suffering? Let us confess our self-righteousness and unbelief and ask for faith, even if it's only the size of a mustard seed. The Holy Spirit truly exists and wants to transform your life into something beautiful. He can take your sorrow, your ashes, and your painful experiences and turn them into something more beautiful than you ever imagined! All you have to do is believe!

If we would humbly ask the Lord to change our desires into his desires and stop living life to meet our selfish cravings, we would see victory here in this life and in the life to come. God doesn't want to set us free only for eternity; he wants us to live free on this earth as well as in the world to come. To be free is to love and serve unconditionally, and if we aren't able to love everyone unconditionally without judgment or prejudice, we aren't free. Love always hopes, and love never puts self first.

Salvation is freely given to all, yet so often our disobedience keeps us from receiving the fullness of our blessings. When we walk in disobedience, we make ourselves susceptible to the Enemy of our souls and the power of evil. All the more reason to choose whom you will serve and to remain steady on the path of righteousness, even through trials and temptations. You must know that the Lord is by your side and is willing and able to set you free from all your afflictions. The psalmist reminds us, "The righteous person may have many troubles, but the LORD delivers him from them all" (Ps. 34:19).

We have been entrusted with God's authority and power to claim victory over our lives. This is possible because Christ, our God, died on the cross, rose from the grave, and has chosen to dwell within us to make us his holy temple. We can go boldly into his holy place to find grace and ask for what we desire, and if we ask anything according to the will of the Father, it shall be granted to us. God's will is that all be restored, renewed, and set free from evil in every form. It is simply a choice and decision that each one must make: *Do you want freedom or bondage?*

Take into consideration that every little decision you make has the potential to have a major impact on your life. The accumulation of little decisions creates the big picture of your decisive will. My hope is that your will might be turned over to the renewing power of the Holy Spirit to wash you, cleanse you, and transform you into perfect love. I wish for you the fullness of God's blessings according to his perfect will, which he has already determined for each of us. May his light reign in your life each and every day.

My journey in life so far has been an incredible adventure. I have gone from an emotionally distraught, lonely, depressed, and hopeless individual to someone who has purpose and an abundance of love deep within me. You, too, are on your own spiritual journey, whether you are aware of it or not.

We are sojourners on this earth, and we will not be here forever. We are like pilgrims in a foreign land. We are on an incredible journey, and every choice we make carries a repercussion for our souls. Our thoughts and actions directly affect the transformations in our minds, perspectives, and emotional states. Ultimately, they shape and direct our will toward the destiny we are choosing for ourselves.

Far too many people are confused and complacent about spiritual matters. Some believe there is a God but mistakenly assume that every "good" person goes to heaven. Others scoff and believe there is no spiritual existence at all. They believe death is a mystery and when the physical body ceases to work, there is nothing. Still others like to imagine that if they do exist after death, they can deal with it, and if there is nothing left, they will never know. They approach eternal life just as they deal with everyday living—by solving problems as they come up and ignoring them the rest of the time.

But the reality of whom you serve and where your soul will spend eternity simply cannot be ignored. My heart grieves to know that so many people will be destroyed by their default decision to ignore the truth of God. There is no way around it. It is the pure in heart who will see God.

Those who choose to seek righteousness as their guide will be filled. We are spiritual beings who will live forever. The word *forever* doesn't have the power or the revelation we need, because everything in this life has an end. We can't humanly grasp "no ending."

I was given the ultimate second chance. And our God is so gracious and merciful that he extends many opportunities for us to know him, turn back to him, love him, and serve him. Don't wait for another chance in your life. Don't wait until it's too late and you find yourself consumed by fire and darkness in a hopeless abyss of despair. Please, please live in the spiritual reality of eternity. Choose to follow Christ Jesus and to serve him with all your heart! Choose the joy of being whole before the glorious splendor of all that is beautiful, holy, powerful, and complete—almighty God. Nothing would give me greater pleasure, my precious friend, than to meet you in heaven one day!

But the choice is yours.

Prayer

If you would like to enter into a relationship with Jesus Christ, please pray this prayer:

Lord Jesus,

I come to you just as I am. I have sinned and I need your forgiveness and restoration. I believe you are the Son of God and that you came to earth to teach us your ways and to die for us on the cross. I believe you were resurrected three days later and offer new life to those who trust in you. Thank you for loving me and for giving me new life by your suffering on the cross. I accept you as the Lord of my life. I understand and thank you that your grace and forgiveness are free gifts and there is nothing I can do to earn them. I ask for the Holy Spirit to come fill me and open my heart and mind as I begin to read the Bible.

In Jesus name, Amen.

If you prayed that prayer, we rejoice with you and recommend you find a local Bible-believing church and consider being water baptized.

We pray that the Lord Jesus will fill your heart with the knowledge of his great love and that you have a heavenly home that is more glorious than you can imagine.

Acknowledgments

In the years since I began sharing my fatal experience, I have seldom satisfied all the questions that arise with such an unbelievable, supernatural encounter. Whether through written materials, a direct audience, or media sources, people desire to know more. So when the opportunity was presented to partner with the nation's leading publisher and one of America's most distinguished authors, I felt compelled to tell my story with even more passion than before. Dudley Delffs, a bestselling author, provided the perspective and insight to aid in the creation of this manuscript. Dudley has become a trusted friend, and his literary talent is deeply appreciated. Dudley, your passion is felt on every page. Likewise, the entire Emanate team is much appreciated. Joel Kneedler is a person I have grown to admire and his belief and dedication to this project is genuinely cherished. Thank you for believing in my story and helping make an impact for the kingdom of God.

Acknowledgments

I want to express a profound gratitude to my family for faithfully standing by me every step of the way. A thank you doesn't seem to be enough for your innumerable sacrifices and unending support.

A special recognition is due to my husband, Rodney, for your constant encouragement and companionship. I am forever grateful that God has blessed me with three incredible children, Chris, Nicole, and Danielle. You are the precious gifts God has given to teach me more about his never-ending love.

To all my precious friends who devotedly prayed and spoke God's Word over my life, I thank you. Most important, I thank my Lord, Jesus Christ, for the humble opportunity to share of his abundant love and mercy.

About the Author

Tamara Laroux is an author, speaker, and cofounder of Life Change International along with her husband, Rodney. Together they have had the joy of sharing the gospel of Jesus Christ in more than forty countries and through numerous media outlets. Tamara is a passionate Bible teacher who loves sharing the truth about Jesus Christ with the brokenhearted. Tamara and Rodney, along with their three children, live in Houston, Texas.